Books in the ABICS Publications Series

Badiru, Deji, **My Little Blue Book of Project Management: What, When, Who, and How**, iUniverse, Bloomington, Indiana, USA, 2014

Badiru, Deji, **8 by 3 Model of Time Management: Balancing Work, Home, and Leisure**, iUniverse, Bloomington, Indiana, USA, 2013

Badiru, Deji, **Badiru's Equation of Success: Intelligence, Common Sense, and Self-discipline**, iUniverse, Bloomington, Indiana, USA, 2013

Badiru, Iswat and Deji Badiru, **Isi Cookbook: Collection of Easy Nigerian Recipes**, iUniverse, Bloomington, Indiana, USA, 2013

Badiru, Deji and Iswat Badiru, **Physics in the Nigerian Kitchen: The Science, the Art, and the Recipes**, iUniverse, Bloomington, Indiana, USA, 2013.

Badiru, Deji, **Physics of Soccer: Using Math and Science to Improve Your Game**, iUniverse, Bloomington, Indiana, USA, 2010.

Badiru, Deji, **Getting things done through project management**, iUniverse, Bloomington, Indiana, USA, 2009.

ABICS Publications

A Division of
AB International Consulting Services (ABICS)

www.ABICSPublications.com

Books for home, work, and leisure

My Little Blue Book of Project Management

What, Where, When, Who, and How

DEJI BADIRU

iUniverse LLC
Bloomington

MY LITTLE BLUE BOOK OF PROJECT MANAGEMENT
WHAT, WHERE, WHEN, WHO, AND HOW

iUniverse books may be ordered through booksellers or by contacting:

iUniverse
1663 Liberty Drive
Bloomington, IN 47403
www.iuniverse.com
1-800-Authors (1-800-288-4677)

Because of the dynamic nature of the Internet, any web addresses or links contained in this book may have changed since publication and may no longer be valid. The views expressed in this work are solely those of the author and do not necessarily reflect the views of the publisher, and the publisher hereby disclaims any responsibility for them.

Any people depicted in stock imagery provided by Thinkstock are models, and such images are being used for illustrative purposes only.
Certain stock imagery © Thinkstock.

ISBN: 978-1-4917-2568-9 (sc)
ISBN: 978-1-4917-2569-6 (e)

Library of Congress Control Number: 2014903710

Printed in the United States of America.

iUniverse rev. date: 03/04/2014

DEDICATION

This book is dedicated to the memory of my dearly departed friend, Mr. Michael O. Adedeji (Busco), who never shied away from any project execution.

CONTENTS

PREAMBLE

My Little Blue Book of project management presents a concise and succinct guide for managing projects at home, work, or leisure. It is, indeed, a little blue book. Both personal and corporate projects can benefit from the contents of the book, although the primary focus is on personal projects at home. We tend to be more organized at work than we are at home. Thus, a book focusing on applying project management at home is very much needed. The essential elements of project management are presented in My Little Blue of Project Management, where the common thread for managing any type of project, both big and small, is the personal commitment of the humans to the project at hand. Regardless of the efficacy of the computer tools and analytical techniques available for project management, the underlying foundation for success, in the premise of this book, is personal commitment. If the most effective tools are not used promptly and properly, no amount of wishful practices and corrective actions can make a precarious project successful. My Little Blue Book of project management advocates preempting project problems through advance planning, organizing, resource allocation, scheduling, and control of project activities.

For ease of reference, My Little Blue Book of Project Management is organized in seven topical areas of What, Why, Who, Where, When, Which, and How.

MEET THE AUTHOR

Adedeji Badiru (pen name Deji Badiru) is a Professor of Systems Engineering at the Air Force Institute of Technology. He was previously professor and department head of Industrial & Information Engineering at the University of Tennessee in Knoxville. Prior to that, he was professor of industrial engineering and Dean of University College at the University of Oklahoma. He is a registered professional engineer (PE), a certified Project Management Professional (PMP), a Fellow of the Institute of Industrial Engineers, and a Fellow of the Nigerian Academy of Engineering. He holds BS in Industrial Engineering, MS in Mathematics, and MS in Industrial Engineering from Tennessee Technological University, and Ph.D. in Industrial Engineering from the University of Central Florida. His areas of interest include mathematical modeling, project systems modeling and control, economic analysis, systems engineering, and efficiency/productivity analysis & improvement. He is the author of over 20 technical books and non-technical guide books. He is a member of several professional associations and several scholastic honor societies.

Deji Badiru has won several awards for his teaching, research, and professional accomplishments. He is the recipient of the 2009 Dayton Affiliate Society Council Award for Outstanding Scientists and Engineers in the Education category with a commendation from the 128th Senate of Ohio. He also won 2010 IIE/Joint Publishers Book-of-the-Year Award for co-editing The Handbook of Military Industrial Engineering. He also won 2010 ASEE John Imhoff Award for his global contributions to Industrial Engineering Education, the 2011 Federal Employee of the Year Award in the Managerial Category from the International Public Management Association, Wright Patterson Air Force Base, the 2012 Distinguished

Deji Badiru

Engineering Alum Award from the University of Central Florida, and the 2012 Medallion Award from the Institute of Industrial Engineers for his global contributions in the advancement of the profession. In February 2013, he led a team that won the Air Force's Air University's 2013 award for Cost Conscious Culture (C3) for saving his department over $300,000 in 2012 operational costs.

CHAPTER 1

What is Project Management?

Project management is everything. Everything is project management. Every human endeavor is, indeed, a project. Everybody is engaged in one type of project or another. Thus, everybody needs project management. But, what is project management? Tools aside, project management is nothing more than a personal commitment to do what needs to be done when it needs to be done and doing it right the first time. Regardless of whatever tools and resources are available, if the personal commitment to execute a project does not exist, then project success will be elusive. Many projects fail because of over-reliance on tools rather than self-commitment. Project management keeps any project moving forward. The what, who, where, when, which, why, and how of any project can be addressed with a disciplined project management approach.

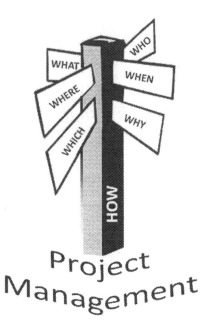

Using the questioning framework, some of the questions that should be asked about a proposed project include the following

- What is the objective of the project?
- Why is the project needed?
- Who will work on the project?
- How will the project be performed?
- Where will the project be performed?
- When will the project start?
- When will the project be completed?
- When will the project be delivered?
- How much will the project cost?
- How will the project quality be managed?

In some cases, a rigorous assessment of the questions above may reveal that the project is not needed at all, thereby saving money, time, and effort. In assessing the project objective, it is essential to evaluate the following questions.

What is the objective?

Does the objective fit into one of the following categories?

- Cost saving.
- Time saving.
- Public relation.
- Market share.
- Service improvement.
- Process improvement.
- Product introduction.
- Political necessity.

If the objective of the project is justified, then the following questions may be asked.

- Do you have adequate resources for the project?
- Do you have enough time to execute the project?
- Do you have a motivation for the project?
- Are there stakeholders for the project?
- Is there sufficient interest in the project?
- Where and how do I fit into the project?
- How do we share resources on the project?
- When is the project to be done?
- Which options are available for executing the project?

Traditionally, a project is defined as "a unique, one-of-a-kind endeavor with a definite beginning and a definite end." This is a limiting definition as it tends to focus on physical products, such as in the construction industry. In the past, this definition made many practitioners to shy away from applying conventional project management tools and techniques to non-construction projects. Indeed, the original applications of project scheduling tools, including the Critical Path Method (CPM) and Project Evaluation and Review Technique (PERT) were more restrictive. Things have changed in recent years as more liberal definitions of a project have become widely adopted; thus, opening the avenues for applying project management to both corporate-focused and home-based projects. For the purpose of this book, I offer the following definition

"A project is any human endeavor intended to produce a product, a service, or a result."

The above view of a project means that everything that we do is, indeed, a project. There are small projects and there are huge projects. They are all, nonetheless, projects that deserve rigorous and dedicated approaches to execute. Based on the above understanding, the following definition of project management is advocated by this book.

"Project management is the process of managing, allocating, and timing resources to achieve a given goal in an efficient and timely manner."

Put simply, this means doing what you need to do promptly and well, with the utmost dedication. Even though there are numerous tools and techniques of project management, the focus of this author is always on the dedication aspect of executing a project. Project failures often occur because we tend to over-focus on tools rather than our own inward dedication to getting a job done. For example, as much as a computer-based spreadsheet tool can help you with your number crunching tasks, you still need to demonstrate the dedication to actually sit down and use the tool . . . and use it correctly. Over-reliance on a tool, without explicit human dedication, means that the tool won't get the job done. Project management requires planning, organizing, scheduling, and control.

Project Planning

What is the end result of this project (deliverable)?
When is the deliverable expected?
How long will the project take?
When can the project start?
What resources are available for the project?
Who will make the GO or NO-GO decision for the project?

Project Organizing

Who else will be involved in the project?
What external support is available for the project?
How much time can participants commit to the project?
Are participants interested, willing, and available (IWA) for the project?

Project Scheduling

What is the overall timeline for the project?
When will resources be available for the project?
Is there a benchmark for the project?
What and where are the milestones for the project?

Project Control

Who will control the execution of the project?
What are the conditions for terminating the project?
Are there hand-over points in the project?
How would we know when the project is over?
What is the time frame for feedback during the project?

In essence, good project management implies coordinating activities so that functions work better together with less waste, better performance, and less expenditure of resources. A good foundation for project management should be devoid of whatever specific tools are available to manage projects. But, using the right tool for the right job saves a lot o time and effort. Our forefathers never had access to today's computer-based tools of project management, yet they successfully managed complex and wide-sweeping projects. With our modern tools, we have an opportunity to enhance the success of project management. Yet, we often hear of major project failures in the private, public, business, industry, and government sectors. Why? Why can't all projects be successful? I argue that most of the obstacles to successful project management can be traced to the soft side (i.e., human elements) of managing projects. This means that, regardless of technical tools, personal commitment, personal attributes, and fortitude are essential for managing projects successfully, whether personal projects or corporate projects.

Attributes of a Project Manager

Good project managers should have the following personal characteristics, at adequate respective levels of attainment.

Personal commitment
Fortitude
Perseverance
Integrity
Credibility
Knowledge of the project subject matter
Competence
Communication skills
Teamwork
Critical thinking
Responsibility
Time management skills
Conflict management skills
Interpersonal skills
Conflict resolution skills
Problem solving skills
Stress management skills

Project Lifecycle

Every project has a life. Sometimes we do better in one segment of the lifecycle than we do in some others. Knowing the various parts and components of your project will give you a better handle on managing the project better. Below is a general profile of a typical project. Specificity will prevail in each project of interest.

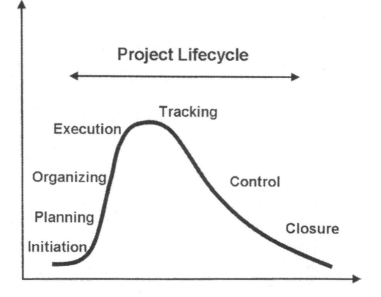

Depending on the nature and size of the project, some of the illustrated elements of the lifecycle may not be applicable while others, such as testing and documentation, may be explicitly required elements. In my opinion, project closure is as important as project initiation. If a project is not closed properly, it may adversely impact other subsequent projects or it may spread its unending tentacles to continue to consume time and resources.

A good simple example of an improperly closed project is a failure to clean up after a do-it-yourself (DIY) home project. The mess left behind will get in the way of subsequent projects. Similarly, tools that are not properly put away into their normal storage areas will create misdirected searches for the tools when they are needed at some future time.

1. List all the detailed activities in the project.
2. Allocate each activity to a team member.
3. Organize the activities in a linked sequence.
4. Estimate how much each activity will cost.
5. Decide the incremental cost associate with each activity.
6. Determine the time duration of each activity.

Project requirements should be pared down to the bare essentials. A fluff-filled project is a failed project.

Laws of Project Management

Certain rules, philosophies, or "laws" are available to guide human efforts in project management. Some of my favorites are provided below.

Badiru's Project Principles

"To get more done, try and do less."

This may appear to be counterintuitive, but what it says is that you should focus your efforts on the most important projects that you can successfully tackle. You cannot do everything, everywhere, to the same level of success. Nowadays, we plan more, but we always seem to accomplish less. That is because we often plan more than what we can handle.

"Grass is always greener where you most need it to be dead."

The lesson in this Badiru's principle is that problems fester naturally if left unchecked. Personal control must be exercised at the earliest opportunity to preempt problems from occurring in the first place. No problem goes away by itself. Once entrenched, a problem will only get bigger.

Parkinson's Law

"Work expands to fill the available time."

This popular project management philosophy implies that any idle time in a project schedule will create an opportunity for an ineffective utilization of time. People tend to find valueless pursuits to fill their free time.

Peter's Principle

"People rise to the level of their incompetence."

This traditional project management principle encourages us to get the right person into the right job. Unfortunately, people often move up in organizational hierarchies due to longevity and incremental promotion rather than due to their managerial competence to handle the current assignment.

Murphy's Law

"If anything can go wrong, it will."
"Anything that can go wrong will go wrong."
"Whatever can go wrong will go wrong."

This decades-old project management adage, in whatever form it is stated, implies that a preemptive strike is needed for possible project problems. By being realistic that problems can develop, we can be better prepared to resolve problems. For example in a do-it-yourself house painting, if we convince ourselves that paint spills will occur, then we will be properly prepared with drop clothes.

Important Versus Urgent Projects

Project management is not just about managing a project. It is also about selecting the right project to work on in the first place. If an unimportant and non-value-adding undertaking can be avoided, that is good project management to begin with. Pareto distribution tells us that only 20 percent of what we undertake creates 80 percent of the value that we seek.

The quad chart below illustrates the variable decision region overlapping the quadrants of urgent and important, not urgent and unimportant, important but not urgent, and not important and not urgent characteristics of projects. Projects should be undertaken based on how they are characterized in the overall pursuits of the project executor. A misidentified or misplaced project does not make for a successful project management.

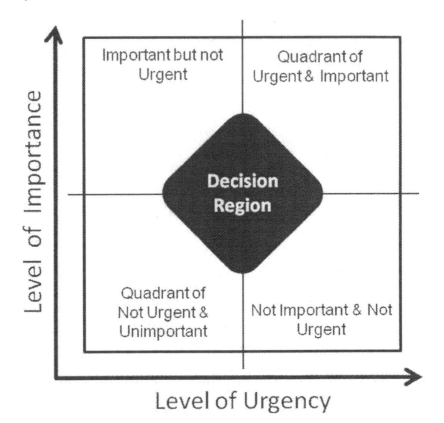

As another good example, practicing defensive driving can help preempt problems that can develop due to road accidents. Accidents, apart from the risk to life and limb, cost a tremendous amount of time and pose a distraction from regular project management efforts. Your ongoing project, whether at home or at work, can easily get derailed if your attention has to be switched from project activities to accident-related activities. If you want to drive fast in response to a pressing urgency, consider the low importance of getting there fast and the risk of not getting there at all.

Project Management Steps

The steps of project management are usually summarized into the five representative stages listed below and shown graphically.

1. Initiation
2. Planning
3. Execution
4. Control
5. Closure

The steps can be contracted or expanded based on the prevailing needs. The steps can also overlap. For example, tracking and control can occur concurrently with project execution. Embedded within execution is activity scheduling. If contracted, there may be only four steps: Planning, Organizing, Scheduling, and Control. In this case, closure is seen as a control action. If expanded, the list may include additional explicit stages such as Conceptualization, Scoping, Resource Allocation, and Reporting.

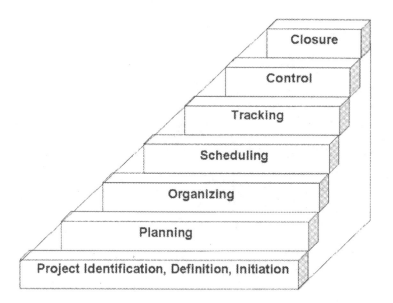

In terms of managing the project time, the project elements are shown pictorially below, flowing from the project initiation through project schedule control.

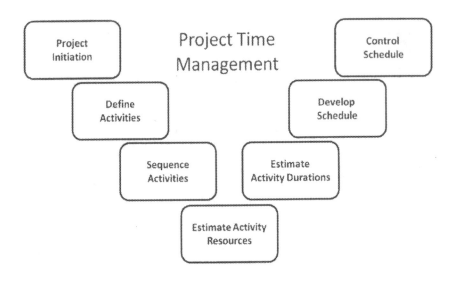

Project Initiation

In the first stage of the project lifecycle, the scope of the project is defined along with the approach to be taken to deliver the desired results. The process of organizing the project is often carried out as a bridge or overlap between initiation and planning. The most common tools used in the initiation stage are Project Charter, Business Plan, Project Framework, Overview, Process Mapping, Business Case Justification, and Milestone Reviews. Project initiation normally takes place after problem identification and project definition.

Project Planning

The second stage of the project lifecycle includes a detailed identification and assignment of tasks. It should also include a risk analysis and a definition of criteria for the successful completion of each deliverable. During planning, the management process is defined, stakeholders are identified, reporting frequency is established, and communication channels are specified. The tools used in the planning stage include Brainstorming, Business Plan, Process Mapping, and Milestones Reviews.

Execution and Control

The most important issue in the execution and control stages of a project lifecycle involves ensuring that tasks are executed expeditiously in accordance with the project plan. Tracking is an implicit component and a prerequisite for project control. For projects that produce physical products, a design resulting in a specific set of product requirements is created. The integrity of the product is assured through prototypes, validation, verification, and testing. As the execution phase progresses, groups across the organization become progressively involved in the realization of the project objectives. The most common tools or methodologies used in the execution stage include Risk Analysis, Balance Scorecards, Business Plan Review, and Milestone Assessment.

Project Closure

In the closure stage, the project is phased-out or formally terminated. The closure process is often gradual as the project is weaned of resources and personnel are reallocated for other needs. Acceptance of deliverables is an important part of project closure. A common tool for project closure is Project Closure Report.

Elements of Project Hierarchy

The project life cycle involves several dimensions, which must all be coordinated within a hierarchical structure covering the levels below.

1. System level (e.g., a university within a state system)
2. Program level (e.g., specific academic programs within a college)
3. Project level (e.g., curriculum development in a department)
4. Task level (e.g., preparation of self-assessment report)
5. Activity level (e.g., documentation of course folders)

For a personal project, most of the project management efforts will be focused at the task and activity levels. Using a project hierarchical framework in any endeavor has the following advantages.

1. A project framework is documented such that other project teams can replicate the template for other efforts.
2. A project framework that has been proven for corporate projects can be adopted for personal undertakings.
3. A project framework ensures that critical and logical steps in a project effort are not neglected.

A note to note

Project management is often seen as an overhead cost not tied directly to a specific product generation. In fact, the product, service, or result that emanates from a project is, indeed, the direct output of project management.

CHAPTER 2

Why is Project Management Used?

"Our greatest weakness is giving up. The most
certain way to success is to try one more time."

- Thomas Edison

If not project management, what else? Project management is needed to ensure that what is intended as an end result is, indeed, what is obtained. Project management ensures responsibility, consistency, and accountability in the pursuit of goals. Project management makes activities tractable. Project management is needed for the purpose of accomplishing goals and objectives. This is why project management is needed so that we don't give up too soon.

Every good opportunity creates new problems to be solved. Life is, thus, a series of opportunities, problems, challenges, and solutions. A person winning $500 million lottery jackpot solves only one dimension of his or her problems, that of money. Several stressful problems and challenges will emanate from the lottery jackpot. Many of such problems are unanticipated and not prepared for. Therefore, they are difficult to solve without the aid of a disciplined application of project management. Project management is needed to pursue opportunities, tackle problems, address challenges, and execute solutions.

Managing expectations and controlling urges are essential in coping with opportunities and challenges. The structured steps of project management make it possible to manage expectations and control urges.

Project management is used for the purpose of impacting structure, sanity, and logic to any endeavor. This is aptly conveyed by the project template presented below. The project outline provides a guide for determining the key elements that go into managing any type and level of a project. The outline can be expanded or collapsed to fit the specific needs and the prevailing circumstances of any project, large or small, corporate or domestic. Not all the line items in the template will be applicable or logical for all projects.

1. Planning

I. Specify Project Background
    a. Define current situation and process
        1. Understand the process
        2. Identify important variables
        3. Quantify variables
    b. Identify areas for improvement
        1. List and explain areas
        2. Study potential strategy for solution
II. Define unique terminologies relevant to the project
        1. Industry-specific terminologies
        2. Company-specific terminologies
        3. Project-specific terminologies
III. Define Project goal and objectives
    a. Write a mission statement
    b. Solicit inputs and ideas from personnel
    c. Develop Statement of Work (SOW)
IV. Establish performance standards
    a. Schedule
    b. Performance
    c. Cost
V. Conduct formal project feasibility
    a. Determine impact on cost

    b. Determine impact on organization
    c. Determine project deliverables
  VI. Secure management support

2. Organizing

  I. Identify project-management team
    a. Specify project-organization structure
      1. Matrix structure
      2. Formal and informal structures
      3. Justify structure
    b. Specify departments to be involved and key personnel
      1. Purchasing
      2. Materials management
      3. Engineering, design, manufacturing, etc.
    c. Define project-management responsibilities
      1. Select project manager
      2. Write project charter
      3. Establish project policies and procedures
  II. Implement Triple C Model
    a. Communication
      1. Identify communication interfaces
      2. Use a communication Matrix
    b. Cooperation
      1. Outline cooperation requirements
    c. Coordination
      1. Develop work-breakdown structure
      2. Assign task responsibilities
      3. Develop responsibility chart

3.Scheduling and Resource Allocation

  I. Develop master schedule
    a. Estimate task duration
    b. Identify task-precedence requirements
      1. Technical precedence
      2. Resource-imposed precedence

3. Procedural precedence

c. Use common project management tools

1. CPM

2. PERT

3. Gantt chart

4.Tracking, Reporting, and Control

I. Establish guidelines for tracking, reporting, and control

a. Define data requirement

1. Data categories

2. Data characterization

3. Measurement scales

b. Develop data documentation

1. Data-update requirements

2. Data-quality control

3. Establish data-security measures

II. Categorize control points

a. Schedule audit

1. Activity network and Gantt charts

2. Milestones

3. Delivery schedule

b. Performance audit

1. Employee performance

2. Product quality

c. Cost audit

1. Cost-containment measures

2. Percent completion versus budget depletion

III. Identify and implement control actions

IV. Phase-out the project

a. Performance review

b. Strategy for follow-up projects

c. Personnel retention and releases

V. Document project and submit final report

The summary lesson from the project execution template is that taking on more than you can handle within the available time, will only lead to failures, disappointments, and frustration. We should always use an incremental approach to accomplish each stage and milestone toward the final goal. Yes, you can be "Jack of 'best' trades," picking only the best efforts to attempt. Yes, you can be a self-actuating project manager to get things done at the level you never thought possible. Project management makes this to be possible and to become a reality.

Project Charter

In the business world, a project charter is used to give notice of a project. The project charter is primarily an announcement of the project and all its ramifications. It establishes the project manager's right to make decisions about how the project will be executed. The project charter summarizes the requirements, management, and financial aspects of a project. It outlines the scope, objectives, benefits, costs, and those involved in the project. Although, one would not need to develop a formal charter for personal projects, it helps to have an understanding of what a charter entails and use that understanding to guide decisions pertaining to personal projects. If nothing else, a conceptualization of the project charter creates an awareness of who is involved and who will be impacted by specific actions that we take in personal day-to-day decisions and activities.

In organizational projects, the purpose of a project charter is to empower the project team and demonstrate management support for the project and the project manager. A charter can also be used by the sponsor to provide general direction for the project and delineate requirements. The charter normally precedes other project documents. It establishes the project manager's authority for the project. Stakeholder agreements are also often based on the contents of the project charter. It is important to do the following when developing or contemplating project charters:

- Recognize key elements of a project charter.
- Understand the use of a charter.
- Appreciate the benefits and pitfalls of developing a charter.
- Leverage teamwork. Teamwork works best.

In summary, a project charter has the following benefits.

- Clarifying business goals
- Defining objectives and scope
- Getting buy-in from stakeholders
- Devising a strategy for managing the project
- Establishing team roles and responsibilities
- Establishing a timeline
- Identifying required resources
- Identifying potential risks

Primary elements of a project charter include.

- Purpose
- Scope
- Goals
- Plan

Define Purpose of the Project

What is your Purpose?
Can you make a business or personal case for your project?
Is there a need for the project?
Can you clearly explain the need for the project in a few words?
Where does it fall relative to your other projects and goals?

Specify Scope of the Project

- Identify what you and your team will focus on for the project.
  - o Task Analysis
  - o Work Design
  - o Redesign of Requirements
  - o Tool and Technology Usage
- Focus on what is important
- Establish limits so that the project is manageable
- Keep the project aligned with expectations and available resources
- Be specific – The more specific the better!!
- Get approval and buy-in from those to be involved (colleagues, family, friends, team members, and so on)

Establish Goals of the Project

- What are your targets?
- How much variability is acceptable?
- How much risk is reasonable?
- Can you measure your effectiveness?
- When do you plan on achieving the goals?

Develop a Plan for the Project

- Outline Project Elements and Milestones
    - List all major activities
    - Estimate duration from start to end
    - Identify resources
    - Identify deliverables
- **Implement the plan**
    - Measure progress and identify corrective actions
    - Show and maintain direction
    - Justify resources
    - Communicate to shareholders
    - Ensure you stay on time budget
    - Ensure results
    - Periodically reinforce buy-in
- **Utilize Sources of Information**
    - Listen to the voice of your constituents or clients. Examples are
    - Voice Of Client (VOC)
    - Voice Of Associates (VOA)
    - Voice of Family (VOF)
    - Transform client requirements into objective measures.
    - Perform a gap analyses of where deficiencies exist.
    - Assess the risk of not meeting goals and the risk of undertaking the project.
- **Use Project Charter Effectively**
    - A project charter can be very effective for managing a project.
    - Use project charter to provide focus on what is important and when things need to be completed.

    o   Avoid spending too much time finalizing the charter. It is a living document and subject to revision as the project progresses.

    o   Periodically revisit and update the charter.

This chapter has presented some of the elements of why project management is needed. Readers can expand and adapt the presentation to their own specific needs and project circumstances.

CHAPTER 3

Who Needs Project Management?

"I like work. It fascinates me. I can
sit and look at it for hours."

- Jerome Klapka Jerome

"Everybody" is who needs project management. Based on his quote above,
Jerome Jerome does need project management. We should not make the
mistake that project management is what is done only in the corporate
environment. Whether at home, work, or leisure, every individual needs
to use project management for his or her pursuits. Project management is
not a grown-up-only pursuit. It is a tool for everyone ranging from kids
to senior citizens. To each embracing project management, his or her own
level of utility applies.

Project management is executed within human organizational
structures. Thus, everyone within the organization needs or uses project
management. The organization structure may be defined in terms of
functional specializations, departmental proximity, standard management
boundaries, operational relationships, or product requirements. In personal
projects, the organization structure may be informal and selected based

on convenience. It is important to communicate the organization chart to everyone involved in the project.

Traditional Formal Organization Structures

Many organizations use the traditional formal or classical organization structures, which show hierarchical relationships between individuals or teams of individuals. Traditional formal organizational structures are effective in service enterprises because groups with similar functional responsibilities are clustered at the same level of the structure. A formal organizational structure represents the officially sanctioned structure of a functional area. An informal organizational structure, on the other hand, develops when people organize themselves in an unofficial way to accomplish a project objective. The informal organization is often very subtle in that not everyone in the organization is aware of its existence. Both formal and informal organizations exist within every project. Positive characteristics of the traditional formal organizational structure include the following.

- Availability of broad manpower base
- Identifiable technical line of control
- Grouping of specialists to share technical knowledge
- Collective line of responsibility
- Possibility of assigning personnel to several different projects
- Clear hierarchy for supervision
- Continuity and consistency of functional disciplines
- Possibility for the establishment of departmental policies, procedures, and missions.

However, the traditional formal structure does have some negative characteristics as summarized below.

- No one individual is directly responsible for the total project
- Project-oriented planning may be impeded
- There may not be a clear line of reporting up from the lower levels
- Coordination is complex

- A higher level of cooperation is required between adjacent levels
- The strongest functional group may wrongfully claim project authority.

Functional Organization

The most common type of formal organization is known as the functional organization, whereby people are organized into groups dedicated to particular functions. Depending on the size and the type of auxiliary activities involved, several minor, but supporting, functional units can be developed for a project. Projects that are organized along functional lines normally reside in a specific department or area of specialization. The project home office or headquarters is located in the specific functional department. The advantages of a functional organization structure are presented below.

- Improved accountability
- Discernible lines of control
- Flexibility in manpower utilization
- Enhanced comradeship of technical staff
- Improved productivity of specially skilled personnel
- Potential for staff advancement along functional path
- Ability of the home office to serve as a refuge for project problems.

The disadvantages of a functional organization structure include the following.

- Potential division of attention between project goals and regular functions
- Conflict between project objectives and regular functions
- Poor coordination similar project responsibilities
- Unreceptive attitudes on the part of the surrogate department
- Multiple layers of management
- Lack of concentrated effort.

Product Organization

Another approach to organizing a project is to use the end product or goal of the project as the determining factor for personnel structure. This is often referred to as pure project organization or simply project organization. The project is set up as a unique entity within the parent organization. It has its own dedicated technical staff and administration. It is linked to the rest of the system through progress reports, organizational policies, procedures, and funding. The interface between product-organized projects and other elements of the organization may be strict or liberal, depending on the organization.

The product organization is common in industries that have multiple product lines. Unlike the functional, the product organization decentralizes functions. It creates a unit consisting of specialized skills around a given project or product. Sometimes referred to as a team, task force, or product group, the product organization is common in public, research, and manufacturing organizations where specially organized and designated groups are assigned specific functions. A major advantage of the product organization is that it gives the project members a feeling of dedication to and identification with a particular goal.

A possible shortcoming of the product organization is the requirement that the product group be sufficiently funded to be able to stand alone. The product group may be viewed as an ad hoc unit that is formed for the purpose of a specific goal. The personnel involved in the project are dedicated to the particular mission at hand. At the conclusion of the mission, they may be reassigned to other projects. Product organization can facilitate the most diverse and flexible grouping of project participants. It has the following advantages.

- Simplicity of structure
- Unity of project purpose
- Localization of project failures
- Condensed and focused communication lines
- Full authority of the project manager
- Quicker decisions due to centralized authority

- Skill development due to project specialization
- Improved motivation, commitment, and concentration
- Flexibility in determining time, cost, performance trade-offs
- Project team's reporting directly to one project manager or boss,
- Ability of individuals to acquire and maintain expertise on a given project.

The disadvantages of product organization are

- Narrow view on the part of project personnel (as opposed to a global organizational view)
- Mutually exclusive allocation of resources (one worker to one project)
- Duplication of efforts on different but similar projects
- Monopoly of organizational resources
- Worker concern about life after the project
- Reduced skill diversification.

One other disadvantage of the product organization is the difficulty supervisors have in assessing the technical competence of individual team members. Since managers are leading people in fields foreign to them, it is difficult for them to assess technical capability. Many major organizations have this problem. Those who can talk a good game and give good presentations are often viewed by management as knowledgeable, regardless of their true technical capabilities.

Matrix Organization Structure

People are often organized in a matrix structure, where everyone brings something to the project depending on respective skills, resources, and talents. The matrix organization is a frequently-used organization structure in industry. It is used where there is multiple managerial accountability and responsibility for a project. It combines the advantages of the traditional structure and the product organization structure. The hybrid configuration of the matrix structure facilitates maximum resource utilization and increased performance within time, cost, and performance constraints. There are usually two chains of command involving both horizontal and vertical reporting lines. The horizontal line deals with the functional line of responsibility while the vertical line deals with the project line of responsibility.

Advantages of matrix organization include the following.

- Good team interaction
- Consolidation of objectives
- Multilateral flow of information
- Lateral mobility for job advancement
- Individuals have an opportunity to work on a variety of projects
- Efficient sharing and utilization of resources
- Reduced project cost due to sharing of personnel
- Continuity of functions after project completion
- Stimulating interactions with other functional teams
- Functional lines rally to support the project efforts
- Each person has a "home" office after project completion
- Company knowledge base is equally available to all projects.

Some of the disadvantages of matrix organization are summarized below.

- Matrix response time may be slow for fast-paced projects
- Each project organization operates independently
- Overhead cost due to additional lines of command
- Potential conflict of project priorities
- Problems inherent in having multiple bosses
- Complexity of the structure.

Traditionally, industrial projects are conducted in serial functional implementations such as research and development, engineering, manufacturing, and marketing. At each stage, unique specifications and work patterns may be used without consulting the preceding and succeeding phases. The consequence is that the end product may not possess the original intended characteristics. For example, the first project in the series might involve the production of one component while the subsequent projects might involve the production of other components. The composite product may not achieve the desired performance because the components were not designed and produced from a unified point of view. The major appeal of matrix organization is that it attempts to provide synergy within groups in an organization.

Project Feasibility Analysis

Human activities are justified and guided by a feasibility analysis. Everyone, whose activities are feasible, needs project management to execute the activities successfully. The feasibility of a project can be ascertained in terms of technical factors, economic factors, or both. A feasibility study is documented with a report showing all the ramifications of the project and should be broken down into the following categories.

Technical feasibility: "Technical feasibility" refers to the ability of the process to take advantage of the current state of the technology in pursuing further improvement. The technical capability of the personnel as well as the capability of the available technology should be considered.

Managerial feasibility: Managerial feasibility involves the capability of the infrastructure of a process to achieve and sustain process improvement. Management support, employee involvement, and commitment are key elements required to ascertain managerial feasibility.

Economic feasibility: This involves the ability of the proposed project to generate economic benefits. A benefit-cost analysis and a breakeven analysis are important aspects of evaluating the economic feasibility of new industrial projects. The tangible and intangible aspects of a project should be translated into economic terms to facilitate a consistent basis for evaluation.

Financial feasibility: Financial feasibility should be distinguished from economic feasibility. Financial feasibility involves the capability of the project organization to raise the appropriate funds needed to implement the proposed project. Project financing can be a major obstacle in large multi-party projects because of the level of capital required. Loan availability, credit worthiness, equity, and loan schedule are important aspects of financial feasibility analysis.

<u>Cultural feasibility</u>: Cultural feasibility deals with the compatibility of the proposed project with the cultural setup of the project environment. In labor-intensive projects, planned functions must be integrated with the local cultural practices and beliefs. For example, religious beliefs may influence what an individual is willing to do or not do.

<u>Social feasibility</u>: Social feasibility addresses the influences that a proposed project may have on the social system in the project environment. The ambient social structure may be such that certain categories of workers may be in short supply or nonexistent. The effect of the project on the social status of the project participants must be assessed to ensure compatibility. It should be recognized that workers in certain industries may have certain status symbols within the society.

<u>Safety feasibility</u>: Safety feasibility is another important aspect that should be considered in project planning. Safety feasibility refers to an analysis of whether the project is capable of being implemented and operated safely with minimal adverse effects on the environment. Unfortunately, environmental impact assessment is often not adequately addressed in complex projects.

<u>Political feasibility</u>: A politically feasible project may be referred to as a "politically correct project." Political considerations often dictate the direction for a proposed project. This is particularly true for large projects with national visibility that may have significant government inputs and political implications. For example, political necessity may be a source of support for a project regardless of the project's merits. On the other hand, worthy projects may face insurmountable opposition simply because of political factors. Political feasibility analysis requires an evaluation of the compatibility of project goals with the prevailing goals of the political system.

<u>Family feasibility</u>: As long as we, as human beings, belong within some family setting, whether immediate family or extended relatives, family feasibility should be one of the dimensions of the overall feasibility of a project. This is not normally addressed in conventional project feasibility analysis. But this author believes that it is important enough to be included

as an explicit requirement. For example, a decision to move from one city to another for the purpose of starting a new corporate job should be made with respect to family needs, desires, and preferences.

<u>Project Need analysis</u>: This indicates recognition of a need for the project. The need may affect the organization itself, another organization, the public, or the government. A preliminary study is conducted to confirm and evaluate the need. A proposal of how the need may be satisfied is then made. Pertinent questions that should be asked include the following.

- Is the need significant enough to justify the proposed project?
- Will the need still exist by the time the project is completed?
- What are alternate means of satisfying the need?
- What are the economic, social, environmental, and political impacts of the need?

It is essential to identify and resolve conflicts in project planning early before resources are committed to work elements that do not add value to the final goal of a project.

CHAPTER 4

Where Is Project Management Used

"Lesson learned should be lesson practiced."

- Adedeji Badiru

Project management should be used everywhere for everything. Please, use and repeat project management in all endeavors. Lesson learned on one project should be lesson practiced on every other project. This goes back to the focus on dedication mentioned in the preceding chapter. Dedication is needed everywhere for everything. In as much as dedication is the foundation for good project management, they both go hand-in-hand for everything. While convoluted project management processes will be counter-productive for simple projects, those simple projects still require personal dedication. A simple project, such as painting a vacant room by one person, will not need tools and techniques of CPM or PERT. But it needs the dedication of the painter with respect to getting the right paint color in advance, laying down a drop cloth, procuring the needed brushes in advance, placing the proper ladder where needed, and making an arrangement for cleanup. Simple as the project appears, any miscue in any of the activities involved, can lead to a failure of the project.

By comparison, a large complex project, such as constructing a new bridge, will involve multi-faceted planning, organizing, and coordinating various activities stretching across diverse groups of people, involve hardware and software assets. For this, a multitude of tools and techniques will be needed to execute the project. Within this spectrum of operation, dedication by individuals and teams will be essential. In essence, success is dependent on the level of dedication applied to each project. In summary, I have the following suggestion.

"Use project management everywhere for everything."

It is just a matter of scaling the application to the level of undertaking involved. From every tiny and mundane endeavor to the most complex of endeavors, you need personal dedication to focus on the end goals. That is, you need project management. Some innocuous examples of where project management can be applied in personal endeavors include the following.

- Studying for an examination
- Writing a book
- Moving into a new house
- Participating in a sports event
- Cleaning up a room
- Cooking
- Managing the home kitchen
- Reorganizing a garage
- Cleaning the garage
- Delivering a seminar
- Classroom Teaching
- Rearranging a room
- Hosting a reception
- Managing personal care
- Any do-it-yourself home project
- 4-H project management
- Executing a thesis or dissertation research
- Conducting a science project
- Hosting a wedding reception

- Organizing a birthday party
- Remodeling a home
- Redecorating or painting a room
- Driving (Yes, driving is a project that must be managed efficiently and safely.)

For corporate projects, examples of profitable applications of project management include the following.

- New product design and development
- Functional requirements planning
- Process improvement
- Office renovation
- Product marketing
- Installing a client survey system
- Personnel management
- New product introduction
- Constructing a new bridge
- Expanding a production line
- Building a new assembly plant
- Setting up a new business
- Running a political campaign

In the academic enterprise, project management may appear as a misfit on the surface. The fact is that many academic endeavors can benefit from the application of project management. Some examples include the following.

- Academic curriculum development
- Developing a lesson plan
- Managing research projects
- Laboratory management
- College fund-raising efforts
- Course registration process improvement
- Interdisciplinary alliance across departments
- Introducing a new degree program

······································

CHAPTER 5

······································

When Is Project Management Used?

"Goals are dreams with deadlines."

- G. T. Stevens, Engineering Economist

Use project management at all times, but certainly at the beginning of any new undertaking whether minor or major. This helps to keep goals within focus and deadlines within reach. Project management is needed right from the outset of any endeavor. Don't wait until the midstream of a project when things are not going well before you start thinking of using project management.

Projects that start right end right.

Preemption of project problems is the best way to solve project problems. Consider the following examples.

- The best way to prepare for a move is to start packing up as you are moving in. Does this sound counter-intuitive? Yes, it does; but it works. What this approach says is that you shouldn't bring junk into your new abode because that junk will become a burden later on when you have to move. If you can avoid that self-imposed obstacle, your moving project, whenever it comes up, will be smoother and more successful.

- To lose weight, you need to preempt weight gain in the first place by practicing moderation and food portion control. Weight, once gained, will cost you more time, money, effort, and resources to deal with later on. This means that your project will be impeded.

- The best way to prepare for a crisis is to invest time upfront to prepare for the next crisis. In the human environment, crisis will eventually crop up. Some are big, some are small. Many are even negligible, but in each case, a lack of advance preparation could lead to project failure. Murphy's Law is alive and well in every human existence.

Time is of the essence in making project management work for you. Task management can be viewed as a three-legged stool with the following three main components.

- Time availability
- Resource allocation
- Quality of the result

When one leg is shorter than the others or non-existent the stool cannot be used for its expected purpose.

Time is of the essence in managing any project. Time is a limited non-recyclable commodity. Industry leaders send employees to time management training sessions and continuously preach the importance of completing tasks on time. However, the one area where time management is most crucial is often overlooked and undervalued. That is, personal task management. Task management, by definition, is in itself time management via milestone tracking of important accomplishments and bottleneck identification. There are only 24 hours in a day and one of the goals for everyone is how to most efficiently use those 24 hours. The tendency is for us to sacrifice the time portion of a personal pursuit and still expect the same level of quality of the output. This thought process is flawed and ultimately leads to failure. If a project that normally takes 12 weeks for completion is condensed into 4 weeks, this would represent a time compression of more than 60 percent. If we were to take the task management stool and reduce one of the legs by 60 percent, the stool would topple over. This is the same result, in terms of performance, when activity compression occurs. An analysis of time constraints should be a part of a person's feasibility assessment of his or her timely task responsibilities. Task planning, personal organization, and task scheduling all have a timing component for a successful project management. As a firm believer in project management and efficient use of time, I always remind myself of the importance of time with the poem below.

The Flight of Time (© 2006, Adedeji Badiru)
Time flies; but it has no wings.
Time goes fast; but it has no speed.
Where has time gone? But it has no destination.
Time goes here and there; but it has no direction.
Time has no embodiment; neither flies, walks, nor goes anywhere.
Yet, the passage of time is constant.

Achieving project success is within reach, if one initiates the project correctly from the beginning. All it takes are a few key ground rules and perseverance, such as those listed below.

- Exercise commitment
- Promise only what you can do and deliver
- Exhibit fortitude
- Extend compromise when needed
- Demonstrate selectivity in selecting projects
- Embrace delegation when appropriate
- Display diligence
- Show perseverance
- Team and partner with others through
  - o Communication
  - o Cooperation
  - o Coordination
- Use the right tools
- Time of what is done
- Commit appropriate types and levels of resources

- Outsource what is better done by a specialized expert

Allocation of Time of Day

Maximize the utilization of each available hour of each day. Do, during the day, what you need daylight or working hours to do. Conversely, do not do, during the day, what you don't need daylight or working hours to do. In other words, use daylight hours appropriately to perform tasks that truly need daylight hours and put off until after-hours, those things that can be done at off hours. Similar thoughts apply to cold and warm weather project selectivity.

Outsource tasks for which you have no skills, tools, or time; or from which you do not derive enjoyment or gratification. But you must retain control of accountability for the tasks.

Seasonal Time Crunch

When do we have time to work on a project? The time for a project is when the project first comes up. There is never a better time. Consider the seasonal time crunch that we all love to blame for not being able to execute our projects. If it is the month of December, we claim that it is the holiday period and we are busy with the season's challenges. We then opt to defer the project to the New Year. When the New Year comes in January, we claim that we are just coming out of the busy holiday period and there are still too many things to do. We then defer the project until the New Year settles, perhaps in February. When February comes, we claim that Spring is just around the corner and we defer everything to the Summer period. When summer comes, we give the excuse that we are busy with the several Summer activities that all come up at the same time. So, we opt to defer the project to the Fall season; and the pattern repeats itself again and again. So, when really is the slow period of the year, where we can get on with our projects? There is no such period as a better time. It is an illusion. If we wait for the best "un-busy" time of the year, we may never execute a project. Applying the techniques of project management encourages us to confront our projects whenever they develop, thus, ensuring that there is continuous series of accomplishments.

CHAPTER 6

Which Tool Is for Project Management?

"There is time for everything, and
a season for each activity."

- Ecclesiastes 3:1

The right tool for project management is whichever tool allows each activity to be placed in its rightful place within the network of activities. Every which way is right for project management that is done right. Every tool can be adapted for project management. There are quantitative tools for project management and there are qualitative tools. The most practical tools for project management are the visual-based tools, such as graphical representation of the project schedule to illustrate activity sequencing. Whether a tool is hard (analytical) or soft (managerial), the same level of dedication is needed for an effective use. The way project management is used depends on the context. Project management executed for home projects will follow simpler processes. Project management executed in the corporate environment will follow a more rigid process based on the level of financial and resource accountability associated with corporate projects. Project management must be tailored to whichever way prevails in the operating environment. The key is to leverage every tool at your disposal for project management. There are mundane tools and there are exotic tools. There are strict scientific tools and there are flexible management tools. All are equally applicable within the context of what the user is interested in. In the approach of this author, even mundane practices such as which way a toilet tissue rolls has implication on how much time and effort are needed to get the right dispensing of what is needed. Many time-saving practices, no matter how microscopic, also eliminate frustration. If frustration is eliminated, focus can be on the real goal.

So, is project management a science or an art? In the opinion of this author, it is mostly art, due to the fact that human demonstration of dedication is required to execute a project successfully. Both the artful and the scientific tools are applicable to project management. When analytical tools, such computer software and graphical data analysis, are used, project management can be viewed as a science. Overall, project management represents a co-mingling of art and science. A person who does not have any scientific training or technical skills can still be a good project manager. In this author's recommendation of using project management for domestic tasks, hardly does it in need to involve science. All that is needed is an artful implementation of forthrightness, focus, and dedication to the expectations of what needs to be done.

**"As a tool, project management is
both an art as well as a science."**

Some of the "which" questions applicable to project management include the following.

- Which project aspects are done in-house versus out-sourced?
- Which resource allocation levels are applicable to the project?
- Which best practices are relevant to the project?
- Which projects tasks are on schedule or behind?
- Which elements of project are new?

The Parody of New Element

The popular Internet parody below illustrates when and which way project management should come to the rescue. Various versions of it are available on the Internet. My own favorite is the one by Jose Luis Preza at the web link below.

http://profron.net/fun/Administratium.html (accessed on February 2, 2014)

"Scientists Discover New Element"
- By Jose Luis Preza

"The heaviest element known to science was recently discovered by university physicists. The element, tentatively named "**Administratium**," has no protons or electrons and thus has an atomic number of 0. However, it does have one neutron, 15 assistant neutrons, 70 vice neutrons, and 161 assistant vice neutrons. This gives it an atomic mass of 247. These 247 particles are held together in the nucleus by a force that involves the continuous exchange of meson-like particles called "morons." Since it has no electrons, **Administratium**, is inert.

However, it can be detected chemically as it impedes every reaction with which it comes in contact. According to discoverers, a minute amount of **Administratium** added to one reaction caused it to take over four days to complete. Without the **Administratium**, the reaction occurs in less than one second. **Administratium** has a half-life of approximately three years, at which time it does not actually decay, but instead undergoes a reorganization, in which assistant neutrons, vice neutrons and assistant vice neutrons exchange places. Studies seem to show that the atomic mass actually increases after each reorganization.

Research indicates that **Administratium** occurs naturally in the atmosphere. It tends to concentrate in certain locations such as governments, large corporations, and especially in universities. It can usually be found polluting the best appointed and best maintained buildings. Scientists warn that **Administratium** is known to be toxic and recommend plenty of alcoholic fluids followed by bed rest after even low levels of exposure."

Administratium, if allowed to accumulate at any level of concentration, can easily destroy any positive reactions. Attempts are being made to determine how **Administratium** can be controlled to prevent irreversible damage, but results to date are not very promising. However, **My Little Blue Book of Project Management** offers the following hints on how to overcome **Administratium** and its administrative implements.

- Use project management to plan, organize, and control projects.
- Use tools and techniques of project management to coordinate efforts.
- Identify project goals and scope the project around the goals.
- Use the right tool for the right job.
- Fit the right person to the right function.
- Achieve operational efficiencies in administrative processes by weeding out non-value-adding steps.
- Phase-out projects promptly once the desired goals have been accomplished.

Tools of Project Management

It is important to sequence activities to determine the most effective order to execute them. This is referred to as activity sequencing, which is the key part of project scheduling. Even simple tasks at home such as cooking, doing laundry, house cleaning, and dressing up do require proper sequencing. The usual stress of multi-tasking to accomplish these chores can be mitigated by smooth sequencing. The common graphical tools for activity sequencing include the following.

CPM (Critical Path Method): This is used to graphically determine the critical activities in a project. The contiguous sequence of critical activities, forming the longest path in the project network, determines the project duration.

PERT (Program Evaluation and Review Technique): This extends the technique of CPM to include three time estimates for each activity. The three time estimates are:

- Optimistic duration (a), which represents the shortest possible duration for the activity in question

- Most likely time (m), which represents an estimate of the most likely duration for the activity
- Pessimistic duration (b), which represents an estimate of the worst possible duration outcome for the activity

From the three duration estimates, the expected activity duration (d) is calculated by the formula below.

$$d = (a + 4m + b)/6$$

$$\text{Expected duration} = \frac{\text{Optimist duration} + 4(\text{Most likely duration}) + \text{Pessimistic duration}}{6}$$

The Role of Activity Sequencing

Activity sequencing presents the interactions between activities and their precedence relationships. In order to develop an effective project schedule, the following questions should be addressed.

Which activities must come first?
Which activities must follow which ones?
Can some activities be run in series or parallel?
Can some activities be eliminated?
What type and level of dependency exists among activities?

Activity sequencing requires the following items.

1. **Project Scope Statement** – The Project Scope statement describes the characteristics of the project and boundaries of performance. The project scope statement complements the project charter.
2. **Activity List** – The Activity List shows the list of activities making up the project. Activity sequencing is the structural ordering of the activities in the list. Activity list is a breakdown of the project deliverables into their component activities and provide crucial inputs for constructing the Work Breakdown Structure (WBS).
3. **Activity attributes** – Activity attributes specify the individual characteristics of activities. The attributes are important for scheduling, sorting, and arranging the contents of the project.

Descriptions of activities often include activity codes, related activities, physical locations, responsible persons, assumptions, and constraints.

4. **Milestones** – Milestones indicate points of significant accomplishments in the project. They indicate progress toward the eventual goal of the project.

The common tools and techniques for activity sequencing are described below.

- **Precedence Diagramming Method (PDM)** - PDM is the most widely used network diagramming method for activity sequencing. It shows activity relationships as start-to-start, start-to-finish, finish-to-start, and finish-to-finish. Each activity is represented by a rectangular block, or node, and linked by arrows to show activity-to-activity dependencies.

- **Arrow Diagramming Method (ADM)** - ADM is a network diagramming method in which activities are shown as arrows. It is sometimes called Activity-On-Arrows. The application of ADM is limited to finish-to-start relationships among activities. The sequence in which activities should be performed is shown by joining activity arrows at nodes. If desired, dummy activities (dummy nodes) are included to indicate project starting point and overall ending point.

- **Dependency determination** - Determining the types of dependencies (i.e., precedence relationship) is critical to the development of a project network diagram. The three types of dependencies used to define the sequence among the activities are

  o Mandatory (e.g., technical),
  o Discretionary (e.g., procedural preferences), and
  o External (e.g., imposed requirements).

- **Applying leads and lags** - Using leads and lags allows the logical relationships between activities to be accurately described. A lead allows for bringing forward the next activity or letting it overlap the preceding activity by a given amount of time. A lag allows for delaying the next activity by a given amount of time or project space.

Sequencing can be performed by using project management software, manual techniques, or a combination of both. The end result of activity sequencing is the network diagram that provides a graphical representation of project activities, milestones, objectives, goals, and the order in which they need to be accomplished. It is helpful to widely disseminate the network diagram so everyone can see and understand exactly where each person fits in the overall project scheme.

Activity sequencing results in outputs which assist in scheduling project activities, allocating resources, and assuring explicit documentation for the required project activities.

Below is a question to ponder about pursuing milestones.

Suppose you are 55 years old now. Would you embark on a personal project whose end result is not to be realized for decades to come? Why or why not? Consider the incremental gratification of accomplishing milestone along the way.

Activity Scheduling

Project scheduling is often the most visible step in the sequence of steps of project management. The two most common techniques of basic project scheduling are the Critical Path Method (CPM) and Program Evaluation and Review Technique (PERT). The network of activities contained in a project provides the basis for scheduling the project and can be represented graphically to show both the contents and objectives of the project. Extensions to CPM and PERT include Precedence Diagramming Method (PDM) and Critical Resource Diagramming (CRD). These extensions were developed to take care of specialized needs in a particular project scenario. PDM technique permits the relaxation of the precedence structures in a project so that the project duration can be compressed. CRD handles the project scheduling process by using activity-resource assignment as the primary scheduling focus. This approach facilitates resource-based scheduling rather than activity-based scheduling so that resources can be more effectively utilized.

CPM network analysis procedures originated from the traditional Gantt Chart, or bar chart, developed by Henry L. Gantt during World War I. There have been several mathematical techniques for scheduling activities, especially where resource constraints are a major factor. Unfortunately, the mathematical formulations are not generally practical due to the complexity involved in implementing them for realistically large projects. Even computer implementations of the complex mathematical techniques often become too cumbersome for real-time managerial applications. A basic CPM project network analysis is typically implemented in the following three phases.

- Network Planning Phase
- Network Scheduling Phase
- Network Control Phase.

Network planning: In network planning phase, the required activities and their precedence relationships are determined. Precedence requirements may be determined on the basis of the following.

- Technological constraints
- Procedural requirements
- Imposed limitations

The project activities are represented in the form of a network diagram. The two popular models for network drawing are the activity-on-arrow (AOA) and the activity-on-node (AON). In the AOA approach, arrows are used to represent activities, while nodes represent starting and ending points of activities. In the AON approach, conversely, nodes represent activities, while arrows represent precedence relationships. Time, cost, and resource requirement estimates are developed for each activity during the network-planning phase and are usually based on historical records, time standards, forecasting, regression functions, or other quantitative models.

Network scheduling is performed by using forward-pass and backward-pass computations. These computations give the earliest and latest starting and finishing times for each activity. The amount of "slack" or "float" associated with each activity is determined. The activity path that includes the least slack in the network is used to determine the critical activities. This path also determines the duration of the project. Resource allocation and time-cost trade-offs are other functions performed during network scheduling.

Network control involves tracking the progress of a project on the basis of the network schedule and taking corrective actions when needed. An evaluation of actual performance versus expected performance determines deficiencies in the project progress. The advantages of project network analysis are presented below.

Advantages for communication

- clarifies project objectives
- establishes the specifications for project performance
- provides a starting point for more detailed task analysis
- presents a documentation of the project plan
- serves as a visual communication tool

Advantages for control

- presents a measure for evaluating project performance
- helps determine what corrective actions are needed
- gives a clear message of what is expected
- encourages team interaction

Advantages for team interaction

- offers a mechanism for a quick introduction to the project
- specifies functional interfaces on the project
- facilitates ease of task coordination

Gantt Charts

A Gantt chart is a special type of bar chart that shows a project schedule on a timeline. Gantt charts illustrate the start and finish times of each activity in a project. A project schedule is developed by mapping the results of CPM analysis to a calendar timeline. The Gantt chart is one of the most widely used tools for presenting project schedules. A Gantt chart can show planned and actual progress of activities. As a project progresses, markers are made on the activity bars to indicate actual work accomplished. CPM network and Gantt charts show the critical activities, which indicate areas requiring additional oversight and tight control.

CHAPTER 7

How do I use Project Management?

"Give me six hours to chop down a tree and I will spend the first four sharpening the axe."

- Abraham Lincoln

Abraham Lincoln's quote above aptly describes how a project should be executed. Get your tools and resources ready upfront and you shall have a successful project. Lincoln also said, "I may walk slowly, but I never walk backward."

A steady pursuit using a sharpened tool works every time in project management. The key is to be firm in your conviction for the application of discipline and dedication in your pursuits. Whether you execute your project slowly or fast, moving toward the intended goals is essential for arriving at the end point. The best defense against project chaos is a direct offense. So, direct actions are needed for a good project execution.

Use project management as you like it. How you execute your project is a function of where you are headed. Project management is used the same way that you would use any tool of decision making. Project management is used by directly confronting the challenges that lie along the path of the pursuit of goals.

Prompt attention is how to use project management. Any task postponed will have to compete against more tasks for your time and attention later on. Procrastination is the foundation for project failure. Get in there and do what you must at the earliest opportunity. Whether you use simple tools, complex tools, or not tools at all, rising up to the need with discipline and resolve is how to implement project management.

> **"Tools or no tools, project management
> is implemented with the utmost
> commitment to getting things done.**

Without a commitment, all efforts are for nothing. First, there needs to be a conviction that the goal is essential. Once that is determined, prompt actions must be directed at the efforts for achieving the goal.

The "how-to" of project management centers on the tools of project management. These tools cover both the qualitative and quantitative techniques. My own preference is to focus on the soft or human-based tools first in order to get the project started corrected. Then, bring in the applicable technical tools.

Communication is the Key

Communication is the root of everything else. Communication, cooperation, and coordination (The Triple C) are Essential for getting things done, even where no other participants are involved. It is often said that one should listen to the inner voice. Well, that is, indeed, an example of self-communication. Similarly, self-awareness is an example of self-cooperation. Furthermore, being organized means being well coordinated.

Organizations thrive by investing in three primary resources as outlined below.

- The **People** who do the work,
- The **Tools** that the people use to do the work,
- and The **Process** that governs the work that the people do

Of the three, investing in people is the easiest thing an organization can do and we should do it whenever we have an opportunity. The Triple C model of project management is portrayed below. The model incorporates the qualitative (human) aspects of a project into overall project requirements for a successful execution.

The Triple C model is effective for project control. The model states that project management can be enhanced by implementing it within the integrated functions summarized below.

- Communication
- Cooperation
- Coordination

The Triple C model facilitates a systematic approach to project planning, organizing, scheduling, and control. The Triple C model can be implemented for project planning, scheduling and control purposes for any type of project. Each project element requires effective communication, sustainable cooperation, and adaptive coordination. The basic questions of what, who, why, how, where, and when revolve around the Triple C model. It highlights what must be done and when. It can also help to identify the resources (personnel, equipment, facilities, etc.) required for each effort through communication and coordination processes. It points out important questions such as the following.

- Does each project participant know what the objective is?
- Does each participant know his or her role in achieving the objective?
- What obstacles may prevent a participant from playing his or her role effectively?

Triple C can mitigate disparity between idea and practice because it explicitly solicits information about the critical aspects of a project. The written communication requirement of the Triple C approach helps to document crucial information needed for project control later on.

Project Communication

Communication makes is possible for people to work together. The communication function in any project effort involves making all those concerned become aware of project requirements and progress. Those who will be affected by the project directly or indirectly, as direct participants or as beneficiaries, should be informed, as appropriate, regarding the following.

- Scope of the project
- Personnel contribution required
- Expected cost and merits of the project
- Project organization and implementation plan
- Potential adverse effects if the project should fail
- Alternatives, if any, for achieving the project goal
- Potential direct and indirect benefits of the project

The communication channel must be kept open throughout the project life cycle. In addition to internal communication, appropriate external sources should also be consulted. The project manager must

1. Exude commitment to the project
2. Utilize the communication responsibility matrix
3. Facilitate multi-channel communication interfaces
4. Identify internal and external communication needs
5. Resolve organizational and communication hierarchies
6. Encourage both formal and informal communication links

Types of Communication

- Verbal
- Written
- Body language
- Visual tools (e.g., graphical tools)
- Sensory (Use of all five senses: sight, smell, touch, taste, hearing - olfactory, tactile, auditory)
- Simplex (unidirectional)
- Half-duplex (bi-directional with time lag)
- Full-duplex (real-time dialogue)
- One-on-one
- One-to-many
- Many-to-one

Project Cooperation

The cooperation of the project personnel must be explicitly elicited. Merely voicing consent for a project is not enough assurance of full cooperation. The participants and beneficiaries of the project must be convinced of the merits of the project. Some of the factors that influence cooperation in a project environment include personnel requirements, resource requirements, budget limitations, past experiences, conflicting priorities, and lack of uniform organizational support. A structured approach to seeking cooperation should clarify the following.

- Cooperative efforts required
- Precedents for future projects
- Implication of lack of cooperation
- Criticality of cooperation to project success
- Organizational impact of cooperation
- Time frame involved in the project
- Rewards of good cooperation

Conflict is the gap between expectations and results. When results don't match expectations, a conflict develops. The Triple C approach can help preempt conflicts through clear communication, explicit cooperation, and dedicated coordination. Cooperation is a basic virtue of human interaction. More projects fail due to a lack of cooperation and commitment than any other project factors. To secure and retain the cooperation of project participants, you must elicit a positive first reaction to the project. The most positive aspects of a project should be the first items of project communication. For project management, there are different types of cooperation that should be understood.

Functional cooperation: This is cooperation induced by the nature of the functional relationship between two groups. The two groups may be required to perform related functions that can only be accomplished through mutual cooperation.

Social cooperation: As the joint apples to the right suggest, *if we work together, we will grow together.* Social cooperation implies collaboration to pursue a common goal. This is the type of cooperation effected by the social relationship between two groups. The prevailing social relationship motivates cooperation that may be useful in getting project work done. Thus, everyone succeeds as a part of the group.

Legal cooperation: Legal cooperation is the type of cooperation that is imposed through some authoritative requirement. In this case, the participants may have no choice other than to cooperate.

Administrative cooperation: This is cooperation brought on by administrative requirements that make it imperative that two groups work together on a common goal.

Associative cooperation: This type of cooperation may also be referred to as collegiality. The level of cooperation is determined by the association that exists between two groups.

Proximity cooperation: Cooperation due to the fact that two groups are geographically close is referred to as proximity cooperation. Being close makes it imperative that the two groups work together.

Dependency cooperation: This is cooperation caused by the fact that one group depends on another group for some important aspect. Such dependency is usually of a mutual two-way nature. One group depends on the other for one thing while the latter group depends on the former for some other thing.

Imposed cooperation: In this type of cooperation, external agents must be employed to induced cooperation between two groups. This is applicable for cases where the two groups have no natural reason to cooperate. This is where the approaches presented earlier for seeking cooperation can became very useful.

Lateral cooperation: Lateral cooperation involves cooperation with peers and immediate associates. Lateral cooperation is often easy to achieve because existing lateral relationships create an environment that is conducive for project cooperation.

Vertical cooperation: Vertical or hierarchical cooperation refers to cooperation that is implied by the hierarchical structure of the project. For example, subordinates are expected to cooperate with their vertical superiors.

Whichever type of cooperation is available in a project environment, the cooperative forces should be channeled toward achieving project goals. Documentation of the prevailing level of cooperation is useful for winning further support for a project. Clarification of project priorities will facilitate personnel cooperation. Relative priorities of multiple projects should be specified so that a priority to all groups within the organization. One of the best times to seek and obtain cooperation is during holiday periods when most people are in festive and receptive mood. Some guidelines for securing cooperation for most projects are

- Establish achievable goals for the project.
- Clearly outline the individual commitments required.
- Integrate project priorities with existing priorities.
- Eliminate the fear of job loss due to industrialization.
- Anticipate and eliminate potential sources of conflict.
- Use an open-door policy to address project grievances.
- Remove skepticism by documenting the merits of the project.

Types of Cooperation

Cooperation falls in several different categories. Some have physical sources, some have emotional sources, and some have psychological sources. The most common categories of cooperation include the following:

- Proximity
- Functional
- Professional
- Social
- Romantic
- Power influence
- Authority influence
- Hierarchical
- Lateral
- Cooperation by intimidation
- Cooperation by enticement

Project Coordination

After communication and cooperation functions have successfully been initiated, the efforts of the project personnel must be coordinated.

Coordination facilitates harmonious organization of project efforts. The construction of a responsibility chart can be very helpful at this stage. A responsibility chart is a matrix consisting of columns of individual or functional departments and rows of required actions. Cells within the matrix are filled with relationship codes that indicate who is responsible for what. The matrix helps avoid neglecting crucial communication requirements and obligations. It can help resolve questions such as

- Who is to do what?
- How long will it take?
- Who is to inform whom of what?
- Whose approval is needed for what?
- Who is responsible for which results?
- What personnel interfaces are required?
- What support is needed from whom and when?

Types of Coordination

- Teaming
- Delegation
- Supervision
- Partnership
- Token-passing
- Baton hand-off

Through communication, cooperation, and coordination, we can offer a ***helping hand*** to our colleagues, friends, and team members so as to get our objectives accomplished. One good turn deserves another. As we succeed together with one project, so we shall succeed with another mutual project.

People, Process, and Tools

The Triple C approach facilitates better utilization of project assets, including people, process, and tools. People are the most enduring and sustainable resources for executing a project. Processes can change and tools come and go, but humans provide a platform of consistency. Consequently, project management practices should include the treatment of people a top priority for project success. The Triple C graphic below depicts the interfaces between people, process, and tools in a project environment.

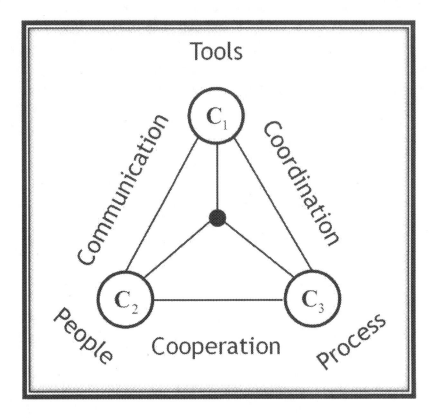

Getting Organized for Project Management

Being organized and staying organized is a key to staying on top of project requirements. The quote below typifies the dangers of inconsistent organization of project resources, consisting of people, tools, and processes.

> "We trained hard, but it seemed that every time we were beginning to form into teams we would be reorganized. I was to learn later in life that we tend to meet any new situation by reorganizing; and what a wonderful method it

can be for creating the illusion of progress while producing confusion, inefficiency and demoralization."

- Petronius Arbiter, 210 B.C.

How to Organize

- First, identify what is needed.
- Then get everything into its own place and return it to its own place after any displacement.
- Move what is not routinely needed out of the way.
- Use the tools and resources at your disposal for project execution.

Think of the early human days of rudimentary development, when everything within reach was used to facilitate survival and growth of the human community.

Take care of your resources

Resources are the basis for executing projects. You must take a good care of your resources so that the resources will be available to serve your project well. Your project resources include yourself. This point is rarely recognized in normal project management processes. If you don't take care of yourself, you won't be able to attend to your project effectively. Proper personal care of yourself means that you will be available to perform your project at the highest level possible. Many little choices that we make about what we do or don't do ultimately affect the execution of our projects. The following are my suggestions.

- Consider yourself as a renewable resource for your projects
- Make healthy personal choices so that you will remain healthy to execute your projects successfully.
- Take care of yourself so that you can take care of your projects.
- Manage your tools for project execution as seriously as you manage yourself.

If personal bad choices are made, they will come back to haunt you and impede your project management requirements. Poor health and sour outlook impede the ability to execute projects efficiently.

Likewise, take care of your means of transportation. Take care of your car so that you can get to where you need to be promptly to do what you need to do in a timely manner. Many projects nowadays depend on accessible modes of transportation. Thus, project implementation can be very car-dependent. Getting to work on time, arriving on time for appointments, and reaching a destination safe all can be impacted by the operational condition of our vehicles. For example, if we get our vehicles ready for harsh winter conditions, we will experience fewer car-related project delays during the winter months. Winter transportation problems can be preempted by doing the following.

- Service and maintain radiator system
- Replace windshield-wiper fluid with appropriate winter mixture
- Check tire pressure regularly
- Invest in replacing worn tires
- Maintain full tank of fuel during winter months to keep ice from forming in the tank and fuel lines
- Have ice scrapers accessible within passenger space in the vehicle; not stored in the trunk

All of the above are common practices that most people are aware of and abide by, but rarely are they explicitly connected to general project management effectiveness.

Japanese 5s Principle for Getting Organized

An African Proverb says, "Tomorrow belongs to those who prepare for it today." Having a good project management experience requires preparing for the project and staying the course. Being organized today paves the way for a successful execution of tasks tomorrow. In the corporate environment, there are formal tools and techniques for organizing work. Those same techniques can be adopted for personal organization. One simple, but rigorous, approach for organizing work is the Japanese technique of 5s, which stipulates workplace discipline through a series of words starting with the letter "s." When five s-words are used, we have "5s" and when six words are used, we have "6s" as outlined below.

1. Seiri (Sort): This means to distinguish between what is needed and not needed and remove the latter. The tools and materials in the workplace are sorted out. The unwanted tools and materials are placed in the Red Tag area, which is used for identifying, tagging, removing, and disposing of items that are not needed in the work area. It applied to the kitchen area in a home, it will mean removing from the kitchen all items not immediately needed in a typical day in the kitchen.

2. Seiton (Stabilize): This means to enforce a place for everything and everything in its place. The workplace is organized by labeling. The machines and tools are labeled with their names and all the sufficient data required. A sketch with exact scale of the work floor is drawn with grids. This helps in achieving a better flow of work and an easy access to all tools and machines.

3. Seison (Shine): This means to clean up the workplace and look for ways to keep it clean. Periodic cleaning and maintenance of the workplace and machines are done. The wastes are placed in a separate area. The recyclable and other wastes are separately placed in separate containers. This makes it easy to know where every component is placed. The clean look of the workplace helps in a better organization and increases the flow of work.

4. Seiketsu (Standardize): This means to maintain and monitor adherence to the first three s's. This process helps to standardize work. The work of each person is clearly defined. The suitable person is chosen for a particular work. People in the workplace should know who is responsible for what. The scheduling is standardized. Time is maintained for every work that is to be done. A set of rules is created to maintain the first 3s's. This helps in improving efficiency of the workplace.

5. Shitsuke (Sustain): This means to follow the rules to keep the workplace 5s-compliant to "maintain the gain." Once the previous

4s's are implemented some rules are developed for sustaining the other S's.

6. Safety: This refers to eliminating hazards in the work environment. The sixth "s" is added so that focus could be directed at safety within all improvement efforts. This is particularly essential in high-risk and accident-prone environments. This sixth extension is often debated as a separate entity because safety should be implicit in everything we do. Besides, the Japanese word for Safety is "Anzen," which does not follow the "s" rhythm. Going further out on a limb, some practitioners even include additional levels of "s." So, we could have 8s with the addition of Security and Satisfaction.

7. Security: This could involve job security, personal security, mitigation of risk, capital security, intellectual security, property security, information security, asset security, equity security, product brand security, and so on.

8. Satisfaction: This could include personal satisfaction, employee satisfaction, morale, job satisfaction, sense of belonging, and so on.

If 5s is practiced with the seriousness of a corporate entity, a better management of projects can be achieved. There is a lot of waste in our normal personal day-to-day activities. These wastes consume time in terms of tracking, storing, and maintaining items. A waste is anything other than the minimum amount of equipment, materials, raw materials, parts, and storage space, which are definitely essential in adding value to work in progress. For example, in a kitchen, maintaining two sets of pots in the immediate vicinity of the stove constitutes a waste, which ultimately translates to time inefficiency.

In a corporate setting, the eight deadly wastes are identified as over production, product defects, inventory, excess process, transportation, excess motion, waiting, and under-utilizing resources (e.g., human resources). The same waste assessment should be done for the home-based projects to ferret out inefficient use of time and resources. In summary, to save time, do the following.

- Things that are frequently used should be placed closer to the work bench.
- Things that are occasionally used should be located in the distant vicinity of the work site.
- Things that are rarely used should be placed in storage and out of the way.

In the humble approach of this author, items needed to get ready for work each morning are reviewed, sorted, and placed in reachable locations the night before. For example, matching ties are pre-selected and pre-knotted, if needed.

This Author's Guide to How to De-Clutter

Avoiding clutter implies getting rid of items that impede progress toward a project goal. Below are some suggestions on how to de-clutter your work space.

- Pare down to the essentials.
- Focus on the end goal of each project.
- Realize that items not within sight and not missed are not needed for immediate tasks.
- Focus only what you need and not what you want within your project scope.
- Be disciplined that if you don't need it, you don't need it.
- Never buy something new unless you are sure you don't already have one of it already in your closet, garage, attic, or backyard.
- Never buy something new unless you definitely know where to put it and how to access it for actual usage.
- Don't plan to do yesterday's work today. Each day's task is best done on its own day.
- There is never the best time to do something. The best and right time is when the task comes up to be done the first time.
- If you haven't seen, touched, or used it within your household in 36 months, you don't need it and it can be donated, unless it is a collectible to be maintained for posterity.

Using Self-Management for Project Management

The people associated with any project should be managed and regulated the same way other high-value resources are managed. Taking care of "yourself" is a direct example of human resource management for project management purposes. Proper diet, exercise, and sleep are essential for mental alertness and they positively impact the ability to get things done. Sleep, for example, affects many aspects of mental and physical activities. Sleep more and you will be amazed that you can get more done on your projects. This is because being well rested translates to fewer errors and preempts the need for rejects and rework. The notion that you have to stay up to get more done is not necessarily always true. Likewise, keep fit and get more done. Studies have confirmed that fit kids get better grades in school. Similarly, fit adults have been found to advance more professionally.

Avoiding Management by Bluff

Don't bluff to do what you cannot or will not do. Management by bluff (MBB) is a term coined by this author to describe those who say they will, but never do. Action bluffing is detrimental to good project management. It is not always easy to accomplish what you "bluff" to do. Thus, cutting down on "action bluffing" and being selective with pledges will help streamline the list of things to do. So, stop talking and start doing. This statement suggests the need to move on to the implementation stage of a project rather than an endless debate. Plans formulated so beautifully on paper or articulated in words mean nothing if they cannot be implemented within the scope of project management.

How to Use a Work Breakdown Structure

In addition to the overall strategies for project management, there must be tactical plans for executing specific activities. Project management is about creating the building blocks for reaching the end goal. The tool of Work Breakdown Structure (WBS) is used to execute projects hierarchically. Each element of the WBS represents something that must be done at a given level of a project. WBS facilitates breaking a project up into manageable chunks, which can be executed incrementally. Project partition or segmentation improves overall project control at the operational level. The chart below illustrates how to break down a project into its components parts for more effective hierarchical management of the project.

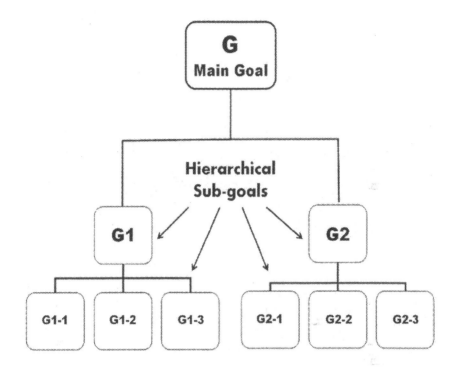

Time-Cost-Quality Tradeoffs

Always weigh cost versus time, cost versus quality, and time versus quality. Preempt problems by using multi-dimensional decision analysis. A simple example is a trade-off decision analysis of traveling by air or by road. The objective here is to get the travel done subject to the nuances of cost, time, and quality; which form the so-called Iron Triangle, shown graphically below.

The concept of Iron Triangle, also known as Triple Constraints, examines the trade-offs between cost, time, and quality or budget, schedule, and performance. Since all three constraints cannot be satisfied at equal levels, a trade-off or compromise must be exercised. As factors of importance in the iron triangle decision analysis, the pros and cons of air travel and road travel are summarized below. Of course, each traveler will have to consider his or her own value streams, risk tolerance level, risk aversion, and goals in the process of making the best decision within the prevailing scenario. Below is a trade-off example for comparing air travel to road travel.

Advantages of Road Air Travel

- Faster
- Statistically safer
- Less tiring

Advantages of Road Travel

- Flexible (depart at your leisure)
- Less travel hassles
- Often cheaper than air fare
- No airport parking worries
- No airport security lines to worry about
- No incidental expenses, car rental, or taxi
- Reduced weather sensitivity
- Ability to pack and take more
- Better meal planning at preferred stopping points
- Ability to take rest stops when needed
- Comfort of the vehicle compared to restricted airplane sitting options
- Pet-friendly
- Protection from unknown seat mates
- No cancellation penalty
- Safety is more within the control of the driver. While flying is said to be statistically safer than driving, there are several things that the road driver can do to increase road safety dramatically.

How to Use a Responsibility Matrix

What is not assigned does not get done; at least not well and not on time. Having successfully initiated the communication and cooperation functions, the efforts associated with the project must be coordinated through an explicit assignment of tasks. Coordination facilitates the organization and utilization of resources. The development of a responsibility matrix (responsibility chart or responsibility table) is essential in every project. A responsibility matrix consists of columns of individuals (actors) and rows of required actions (tasks). Cells within the matrix are filled with relationship codes that indicate who has the responsibility for what. The matrix should indicate the following.

- Who is to do what?
- Who is playing what role?
- Who is to inform whom of what?
- Whose approval is needed for what?
- Who is responsible for which results?
- What personnel interfaces are involved?
- What support is needed from whom for what functions?

A responsibility matrix specifies the interface between activities making up a project as contained in the work breakdown structure and the individuals participating in the project. The larger the project team, the higher the need for a responsibility matrix. For large projects, it is necessary to develop a separate responsibility matrix for each subproject in the work breakdown structure. Common relationship codes for insertion into the cells of the responsibility matrix include the following.

A: Responsibility for Approval
I: Responsibility for Information communication
C: Responsibility for Consultation
D: Responsibility for Data provision
S: Responsibility for providing Support
N: Responsibility for Notification
T: Responsibility for Teaming

Other custom codes may be developed to address specific needs of a particular project. A simple example of a responsibility matrix is shown below. Every task should be assigned as a responsibility to at least one participant (actor) in the project. Every participant included in the responsibility matrix should have at least one responsibility to execute either as an individual or as a team member.

With responsibility comes accountability. A formal application of the tools and techniques of project management is essential for building a consensus of responsibility and accountability. My little blue book of project management has presented a framework for executing project.

	Responsibility			
Actors	Task 1	Task 2	Task 3	Task 4
Person A	R	T		
Person B		R	I	
Person C				R
Person D	A	C		A
Person E	N		R	

Tips for Home Projects

"Success is doing what you can do well
and doing well whatever you do."

- Longfellow

Daylight and Off-daylight Projects

Do during the daylight what you need daylight to do and do off-daylight
what artificial lighting will suffice to do. For example, a discretionary chore
in a lighted basement should not be done during the daylight when the
competing chore of mowing the lawn is waiting. Why? Since the basement
is lighted, the work can be scheduled for any time. Use daylight hours to
do the work that is needed in the kitchen, the garage, or the yard, where
natural light is essential and cost-avoiding.

Being Good and Getting Good Results

This may sound corny. But, in terms of project management, what
goes around comes back around. Being good preempts the need for a
corrective action, which may divert time from meaningful and value-
adding engagements. If you do the right thing up front, you will not have
to spend time to do it again or to make amendments. Blunders committed
in human interrelationships end costing time and resources to amend. Be

good and you will be amazed how much time you can save to be used for other good and rewarding things.

Home Kitchen Management

The kitchen is a central part of any home. This is where most of the domestic activities of a family take place. So, getting the kitchen organized is essential for the success of any family project. Kitchen efficiency and effectiveness can be improved through basic project management approaches. For example, do a "kitchen reset" periodically by using the 5s Principles presented earlier. One approach to sprucing up the efficiency of a kitchen is to pull everything out of the kitchen cabinet. Review and prune the items pulled. Only those items that meet the strict 5s review should be returned to the cabinets. This approach will help keep the kitchen organized, neat, safe, efficient, and effective. A well-organized kitchen means that more time will be available for other crucial projects around the home.

Think "Glocal"

Every project has both a global impact and a local impact. Thinking "Glocal," in the author's own word, means that both the global implications and the local impacts of a project are recognized. A project management framework will recognize the internal and external factors affecting the project.

Using DEJI Model to Justify and Integrate a Project

The author's DEJI model was developed specifically for systems management applications, but it has a direct applicability for the project management process. The model advocates using a mix of quantitative and qualitative tools and techniques to Design the project, Evaluate the project, Justify the project, and Integrate the project.

DEJI Model Components	Characteristics	Tools & Techniques
Design ➡	Define goals Set metrics Identify critical factors	Parametric assessment, project state transition, value stream analysis, etc.
Evaluate ➡	Measure parameters Assess attributes Benchmark	Pareto analysis, risk analysis, lifecycle analysis, etc.
Justify ➡	Economic Technical Alignment with strategic goals	Benefit cost ratio, payback period, present value calculation, etc.
Integrate ➡	Identify common elements Verify symbiosis Check value synergy	Alignment with existing functions, process tightening, etc.

Garage Cleanup Project Tips

Cleaning up the garage is a common project around the home. Basic project management techniques can be applied to favorite but un-favored home project. Again, using the 5s approach can simplify the project. The author recommends using whatever project-enhancing tools are within reach. His favorite tool is an empty plastic water bottle and other plastic see-through cases. The figure below illustrates how the author uses a recycle bottle to restored order to and a tangled cord.

Before

After

Tool

(Recycled empty plastic water bottle)

The author also recycles empty plastic water bottles for filling packages instead of using commercial bubble wraps. The procedure is simple, as summarized below.

1. Completely empty the plastic water bottle.
2. With the bottle cap off, compress the bottle, letting air out, until the bottle reaches the size desired to fill the desired packaging.
3. Replace the cap and tighten it so that air cannot exit or enter the bottle.
4. Place the correctly-sized bottles (however many are needed) in packages to fill gaps. This approach is particularly effective for securing delicate items to be shipped.

The figure below shows another example of the author's use of an empty see-through plastic mixed-nut snack bottle to organize the garage. In this case, miscellaneous light bulbs of different sizes are organized neatly into the plastic bottle. The contents are easily seen and retained compactly and safely in the bottle.

Before   After

To save time on cleaning up, try not to make a big mess in the first place. A clean and organized work space saves time and preempts the need for corrective actions later one.

Glossary of Project Terms

- ABC. Activity Based Costing. Bottom up estimating and summation based on material and labor required for activities making up a project.
- Activity. A component of work performed during the course of & project. See also schedule activity.
- Activity Duration. The time in calendar units between the start and finish of a schedule activity. See also actual duration, original duration, and remaining duration.
- Activity Resource Estimating. The process of estimating the types and quantities of resources required to perform each schedule activity.
- Activity Sequencing. The process of identifying and documenting dependencies among schedule activities.
- Authority. The right to apply project resources, expend funds, make decisions, or give approvals.
- Bar Chart. A graphic display of schedule-related information, fn the typical bar chart, schedule activities or work breakdown structure components are listed down the left side of the chart, dates are shown across the top, and activity durations are shown as date-placed horizontal bars. Also called a Gantt chart.
- Baseline. The approved time phased plan (for a project, a work breakdown structure component, a work package, or a schedule activity), plus or minus approved project scope, cost, schedule,

and technical changes. Generally refers to the current baseline, but may refer to the original or some other baseline. Usually used with a modifier (e.g., cost baseline, schedule baseline, performance measurement baseline, technical baseline). See also performance measurement baseline.

- Best Practices. Processes, procedures, and techniques that have consistently demonstrated achievement of expectations and that are documented for the purposes of sharing, repetition, replication, adaptation, and refinement.
- Change Control. Identifying, documenting, approving or rejecting, and controlling changes to the project baselines.
- Close Project. The process of finalizing all activities across all of the project process groups to formally close the project or phase.
- Common Cause. A source of variation that is inherent in the system and predictable. On a control chart, it appears as part of the random process variation (i.e., variation from a process that would be considered normal or not unusual), and is indicated by a random pattern of points within the control limits. Also referred to as random cause. Contrast with special cause.
- Configuration Management System. A subsystem of the overall project management system. It is a collection of formal documented procedures used to apply technical and administrative direction and surveillance to identify and document the functional and physical characteristics of a product, result, service, or component; control any changes to such characteristics, record and report each change and its implementation status; and support the audit of the products, results, or components to verify conformance to requirements. It includes the documentation, tracking systems, and defined approval levels necessary for authorizing and controlling changes. In most application areas, the configuration management system includes the change control system.
- Constraint. The state, quality, or sense of being restricted to a given course of action or inaction. An applicable restriction or limitation – either internal or external to the project – that will affect the performance of the project or a process. For example, a schedule constraint is any limitation or restraint placed on the project

schedule that affects when a schedule activity can be scheduled and is usually in the form of fixed imposed dates. A cost constraint is any limitation or restraint placed on the project budget such as funds available over time. A project resource constraint is any limitation or restraint placed on resource usage, such as what resource skills or disciplines are available and the amount of a given resource available during a specified time frame.

- Contingency Reserve. The amount of funds, budget, or time needed above the estimate to reduce the risk of overruns of project objectives to a level acceptable to the organization.

- Control. Comparing actual performance with planned performance, analyzing variances, assessing trends to effect process improvements, evaluating possible alternatives, and recommending appropriate corrective action as needed.

- Control Chart. A graphic display of process data over time and against established control limits, and that has a centerline that assists in detecting a trend of plotted values toward either control limit.

- Control Limits. The area composed of three standard deviations on either side of the centerline, or mean, of a normal distribution of data plotted on a control chart that reflects the expected variation in the data. See also specification limits.

- Cost Control. The process of influencing the factors that create variances, and controlling changes to the project budget.

- Cost of Quality (COQ). Determining the costs incurred to ensure quality. Prevention and appraisal costs (cost of conformance) include costs for quality planning, quality control (QC), and quality assurance to ensure compliance to requirements (i.e., training, QC systems, etc.). Failure costs (cost of non-conformance) include costs to rework products, components, or processes that are non-compliant, costs of warranty work and waste, and loss of reputation.

- Cost Performance Index (CPI). A measure of cost efficiency on ^project. It is the ratio of earned value (EV) to actual costs (AC). CPI = EV divided by AC. A CPI value equal to or greater than one indicates a favorable condition and a value less than one indicates an unfavorable condition.

- Cost-Plus-Fee (CPF). A type of cost reimbursable contract where the buyer reimburses the seller for seller's allowable costs for performing the contract work and seller also receives a fee calculated as an agreed upon percentage of the costs. The fee varies with the actual cost.

- Cost-Plus-Fixed-Fee (CPFF) Contract. A type of cost-reimbursable contract where the buyer reimburses the seller for the seller's allowable costs (allowable costs are defined by the contract) plus a fixed amount of profit (fee).

- Cost-Pius-Incentive-Fee (CPIF) Contract. A type of cost-reimbursable contract where the buyer reimburses the seller for the seller's allowable costs (allowable costs are defined by the contract), and the seller earns its profit if it meets defined performance criteria.

- Cost-Plus-Percentage of Cost (CPPC). See *cost-plus-fee.*

- Cost-Reimbursable Contract. A type of contract involving payment (reimbursement) by the buyer to the seller for the seller's actual costs, plus a fee typically representing seller's profit. Costs are usually classified as direct costs or indirect costs. Direct costs are costs incurred for the exclusive benefit of the project, such as salaries of full-time project staff. Indirect costs, also called overhead and general and administrative cost, are costs allocated to the project by the performing organization as a cost of doing business, such as salaries of management indirectly involved in the project, and cost of electric utilities for the office. Indirect costs are usually calculated as a percentage of direct costs. Cost-reimbursable contracts often include incentive clauses where, if the seller meets or exceeds selected project objectives, such as schedule targets or total cost, then the seller receives from the buyer an incentive or bonus payment.

- Cost Variance (CV). A measure of cost performance on a project. It is the algebraic difference between earned value (EV) and actual cost (AC). CV = EV minus AC. A positive value indicates a favorable condition and a negative value indicates an unfavorable condition.

- Crashing. A specific type of project schedule compression technique performed by taking action to decrease the total project schedule duration after analyzing a number of alternatives to determine how to get the maximum schedule duration compression for the least additional cost. Typical approaches for crashing a schedule include reducing schedule activity durations and increasing the assignment of resources on schedule activities. See schedule compression and see also fast tracking.

- Create WBS (Work Breakdown Structure). The process of subdividing the major project deliverables and project work into smaller, more manageable components.

- Critical Activity. Any schedule activity on a critical path in a project schedule. Most commonly determined by using the critical path method. Although some activities are "critical," in the dictionary sense, without being on the critical path, this meaning is seldom used in the project context.

- Critical Chain Method. A schedule network, analysis technique that modifies the project schedule to account for limited resources. The critical chain method mixes deterministic and probabilistic approaches to schedule network analysis.

- Critical Path. Generally, but not always, the sequence of schedule activities that determines the duration of the project. Generally, it is the longest path through the project. However, a critical path can end, as an example, on a schedule milestone that is in the middle of the project schedule and that has a finish-no-later-than imposed date schedule constraint. See also critical path method.

- Critical Path Method (CPM). A schedule network analysis technique used to determine the amount of scheduling flexibility (the amount of float) on various logical network paths in the project schedule network, and to determine the minimum total project duration. Early start and finish dates are calculated by means of and forward pass, using a specified start date. Late start and finish dates are calculated by means of a backward pass, starting from a specified completion date, which sometimes is the project early finish date determined during the forward pass calculation.

- Decision Tree Analysis. The decision tree is a diagram that describes a decision under consideration and the implications of choosing one or another of the available alternatives. It is used when some future scenarios or outcomes of actions are uncertain. It incorporates probabilities and the costs or rewards of each logical path of events and future decisions, and uses expected monetary value analysis to help the organization identify the relative values of alternate actions. See also expected monetary value analysis.

- Decomposition. A planning technique that subdivides the project scope and project deliverables into smaller, more manageable components, until the project work associated with accomplishing the project scope and providing the deliverables is defined in sufficient detail to support executing, monitoring, and controlling the work.

- Defect. An imperfection or deficiency in a project component where that component does not meet its requirements or specifications and needs to be either repaired or replaced.

- Defect Repair. Formally documented identification of a defect in a project component with a recommendation to either repair the defect or completely replace the component.

- Deliverable. Any unique and verifiable product, result, or capability to perform a service that must be produced to complete a process, phase, or project. Often used more narrowly in reference to an external deliverable, which is a deliverable that is subject to approval by the project sponsor or customer. See also product, service, and result.

- Delphi Technique. An information gathering technique used as a way to reach a consensus of experts on a subject. Experts on the subject participate in this technique anonymously. A facilitator uses a questionnaire to solicit ideas about the important project points related to the subject. The responses are summarized and are then re-circulated to the experts for further comment. Consensus may be reached in a few rounds of this process. The Delphi technique helps reduce bias in the data and keeps any one person from having undue influence on the outcome.

- Develop Project Charter. The process of developing the project charter that formally authorizes a project.

- Discrete Effort. Work effort that is directly identifiable to the completion of specific work breakdown structure components and deliverables, and that can be directly planned and measured. Contrast with apportioned effort.

- Dummy Activity. A schedule activity of zero duration used to show a logical relationship in the arrow diagramming method. Dummy activities are used when logical relationships cannot be completely or correctly described with schedule activity arrows. Dummy activities are generally shown graphically as a dashed line headed by an arrow.

- Early Finish Date (EF). In the critical path method, the earliest possible point in time on which the uncompleted portions of a schedule activity (or the project) can finish, based on the schedule network, logic, the data date, and any schedule constraints. Early finish dates can change as the project progresses and as changes are made to the project management plan.

- Early Start Date (ES). In the critical path method, the earliest possible point in time on which the uncompleted portions of a schedule activity (or the project) can start, based on the schedule network logic, the data date, and any schedule constraints. Early start dates can change as the project progresses and as changes are made to the project management plan.

- Earned Value (EV). The value of completed work expressed in terms of the approved budget assigned to that work for a schedule activity or work breakdown structure component. Also referred to as the budgeted cost of work performed (BCWP).

- Earned Value Management (EVM). A management methodology for integrating scope, schedule, and resources, and for objectively measuring project performance and progress. Performance is measured by determining the budgeted cost of work performed (i.e., earned value} and comparing it to the actual cost of work performed (i.e., actual cost}. Progress is measured by comparing the earned value to the planned value.

- Earned Value Technique (EVT). A specific technique for measuring the performance of work for a work breakdown structure component, control account, or project. Also referred to as the earning rules and crediting method.

- Effort. The number of labor units required to complete a schedule activity or work breakdown structure component. Usually expressed as staff hours, staff days, or staff weeks. Contrast with duration.

- Enterprise. A company, business, firm, partnership, corporation, or governmental agency.

- Enterprise Environmental Factors. Any or all external environmental factors and internal organizational environmental factors that surround or influence the project's success. These factors are from any or all of the enterprises involved in the project, and include organizational culture and structure, infrastructure, existing resources, commercial databases, market conditions, and project management software.

- Execute. Directing, managing, performing, and accomplishing the project work, providing the deliverables, and providing work performance information.

- Expected Monetary Value (EMV) Analysis. A statistical technique that calculates the average outcome when the future includes scenarios that may or may not happen. A common use of this technique is within decision tree analysis. Modeling and simulation are recommended for cost and schedule risk analysis because it is more powerful and less subject to misapplication than expected monetary value analysis.

- Expert Judgment. Judgment provided based upon expertise in an application area, knowledge area, discipline, industry, etc. as appropriate for the activity being performed. Such expertise may be provided by any group or person with specialized education, knowledge, skill, experience, or training, and is available from many sources, including other units within the performing organization; consultants; stakeholders, including customers, professional and technical associations; and industry groups.

- Failure Mode and Effect Analysis (FMEA). An analytical procedure, in which each potential failure mode in every component of a product is analyzed to determine its effect on the reliability of that component and, by itself or in combination with other possible failure modes, on the reliability of the product or system and on the required function of the component; or the examination of a product (at the system and/or lower levels) for all ways that a failure may occur. For each potential failure, an estimate is made of its effect on the total system and of its impact. In addition, a review is undertaken of the action planned to minimize the probability of failure and to minimize its effects.

- Fast Tracking. A specific project schedule compression technique that changes network logic to overlap phases that would normally be done in sequence, such as the design phase and construction phase, or to perform schedule activities in parallel. See schedule compression and see also crashing.

- Finish-to-Finish (FF). The logical relationship where completion of work of the successor activity cannot finish until the completion of work of the predecessor activity. See also logical relationship.

- Finish-to-Start (FS). The logical relationship where initiation of work of the successor activity depends upon the completion of work of the predecessor activity. See also logical relationship.

- Firm-Fixed-Price (FFP) Contract. A type of fixed price contract where the buyer pays the seller a set amount (as defined by the contract}, regardless of the seller's costs.

- Fixed-Price-Incentive-Fee (FPIF) Contract. A type of contract where the buyer pays the seller a set amount (as defined by the contract), and the seller can earn an additional amount if the seller meets defined performance criteria.

- Fixed-Price or Lump-Sum Contract. A type of contract involving a fixed total price for a well-defined product. Fixed-price contracts may also include incentives for meeting or exceeding selected project objectives, such as schedule targets. The simplest form of a fixed price contract is a purchase order.

- Float. Also called slack. See total float and see also free float.
- Flowcharting. The depiction in a diagram format of the inputs, process actions, and outputs of one or more processes within a system.
- Free Float (FF). The amount of time that a schedule activity can be delayed without delaying the early start of any immediately following schedule activities. See also total float.
- Gantt Chart. See *bar chart*.
- Imposed Date. A fixed date imposed on a schedule activity or schedule milestone, usually in the form of a "start no earlier than" and "finish no later than" date.
- Influence Diagram. Graphical representation of situations showing causal influences, time ordering of events, and other relationships among variables and outcomes.
- Integrated Change Control. The process of reviewing all change requests, approving changes and controlling changes to deliverables and organizational process assets.
- Invitation for Bid (IFB). Generally, this term is equivalent to request for proposal. However, in some application areas, it may have a narrower or more specific meaning.
- Lag. A modification of a logical relationship that directs a delay in the successor activity. For example, in a finish-to-start dependency with a ten-day lag, the successor activity cannot start until ten days after the predecessor activity has finished. See also lead.
- Late Finish Date (LF). In the critical path method, the latest possible point in time that a schedule activity may be completed based upon the schedule network logic, the project completion date, and any constraints assigned to the schedule activities without violating a schedule constraint or delaying the project completion date. The late finish dates are determined during the backward pass calculation of the project schedule network.
- Late Start Date (LS). In the critical path method, the latest possible point in time that a schedule activity may begin based upon the schedule network logic, the project completion date, and any constraints assigned to the schedule activities without violating a schedule constraint or delaying the project completion

date. The late start dates are determined during the backward pass calculation of the project schedule network.

- Latest Revised Estimate. See *estimate at completion.*
- Lead. A modification of a logical relationship that allows an acceleration of the successor activity. For example, in a finish-to-start dependency with a ten-day lead, the successor activity can start ten days before the predecessor activity has finished. See also lag. A negative lead is equivalent to a positive lag.
- Life Cycle. *See project life cycle.*
- Materiel. The aggregate of things used by an organization in any undertaking, such as equipment, apparatus, tools, machinery, gear, material, and supplies.
- Matrix Organization. Any organizational structure in which the project manager shares responsibility with the functional managers for assigning priorities and for directing the work of persons assigned to the project.
- Milestone. A significant point or event in the project. See also schedule milestone.
- Monte Carlo Analysis. A technique that computes, or iterates, the project cost or project schedule many times using input values selected at random from probability distributions of possible costs or durations, to calculate a distribution of possible total project cost or completion dates.
- Opportunity. A condition or situation favorable to the project, a positive set of circumstances, a positive set of events, a risk that will have a positive impact on project objectives, or a possibility for positive changes. Contrast with threat.
- Organizational Breakdown Structure (OBS). A hierarchically organized depiction of the project organization arranged so as to relate the work packages to the performing organizational units. (Sometimes OBS is written as Organization Breakdown Structure with the same definition.)
- Parametric Estimating. An estimating *technique* that uses a statistical relationship between historical data and other variables (e.g., square footage in construction, lines of code in software development) to calculate an *estimate* for activity parameters, such

as *scope, cost, budget,* and *duration.* This technique can produce higher levels of accuracy depending upon the sophistication and the underlying data built into the model. An example for the cost parameter is multiplying the planned quantity of work to be performed by the historical cost per unit to obtain the estimated cost.

- Pareto Chart. A histogram, ordered by frequency of occurrence, that shows how many results were generated by each identified cause.
- Position Description. An explanation of a project team member's roles and responsibilities.
- Precedence Relationship. The term used in the precedence diagramming method for a logical relationship. In current usage, however, precedence relationship, logical relationship, and dependency are widely used interchangeably, regardless of the diagramming method used.
- Predecessor Activity. The schedule activity that determines when the logical successor activity can begin or end.
- Product Life Cycle. A collection of generally sequential, non-overlapping product phases whose name and number are determined by the manufacturing and control needs of the organization. The last product life cycle phase for a product is generally the product's deterioration and death. Generally, a project life cycle is contained within one or more product life cycles.
- Product Scope. The features and functions that characterize a product, service, or result.
- Product Scope Description. The documented narrative description of the product scope.
- Program. A group of related projects managed in a coordinated way to obtain benefits and control not available from managing them individually. Programs may include elements of related work outside of the scope of the discrete projects in the program.
- Program Management. The centralized coordinated management of a program to achieve the program's strategic objectives and benefits.

- Program Management Office (PMO). The centralized management of a particular program or programs such that corporate benefit is realized by the sharing of resources, methodologies, tools, and techniques, and related high-level project management focus. See also project management office.
- Project. A temporary endeavor undertaken to create a unique product, service, or result.
- Project Charter. A document issued by the project initiator or sponsor that formally authorizes the existence of a project, and provides the project manager with the authority to apply organizational resources to project activities..
- Project Life Cycle. A collection of generally sequential project phases whose name and number are determined by the control needs of the organization or organizations involved in the project. A life cycle can be documented with a methodology.
- Project Organization Chart. A document that graphically depicts the project team members and their interrelationships for a specific project.
- Project Scope Statement. The narrative description of the project scope, including major deliverables, project objectives, project assumptions, project constraints, and a statement of work, that provides a documented basis for making future project decisions and for confirming or developing a common understanding of project scope among the stakeholders. A statement of what needs to be accomplished.
- Resource Leveling. Any form of schedule network analysis in which scheduling decisions (start and finish dates) are driven by resource constraints (e.g., limited resource availability or difficult-to-manage changes in resource availability levels).
- Responsibility Matrix. A structure that relates the project organizational breakdown structure to the work breakdown structure to help ensure that each component of the project's scope of work is assigned to a responsible person.
- Risk. An uncertain event or condition that, if it occurs, has a positive or negative effect on a project's objectives. See also risk category and risk breakdown structure.

- Risk Acceptance. A risk response planning technique that indicates that the project team has decided not to change the project management plan to deal with a risk, or is unable to identify any other suitable response strategy.
- Risk Avoidance. A risk response planning technique for a threat that creates changes to the project management plan that are meant to either eliminate the risk or to protect the project objectives from its impact. Generally, risk avoidance involves relaxing the time, cost, scope, or quality objectives.
- Risk Breakdown Structure (RBS). A hierarchically organized depiction of the identified project risks arranged by risk category and subcategory that identifies the various areas and causes of potential risks. The risk breakdown structure is often tailored to specific project types.
- Rolling Wave Planning. A form of progressive elaboration planning where the work to be accomplished in the near term is planned in detail at a low level of the work breakdown structure, while the work far in the future is planned at a relatively high level of the work breakdown structure, but the detailed planning of the work to be performed within another one or two periods in the near future is done as work is being completed during the current period.
- Root Cause Analysis. An analytical technique used to determine the basic underlying reason that causes a variance or a defect or a risk. A root cause may underlie more than one variance or defect or risk.
- Schedule Milestone. A significant event in the project schedule, such as an event restraining future work or marking the completion of a major deliverable. A schedule milestone has zero duration. Sometimes called a milestone activity. See also milestone.
- Scope. The sum of the products, services, and results to be provided as a project. See also project scope and product scope.
- S-Curve. Graphic display of cumulative costs, labor hours, percentage of work, or other quantities, plotted against time. The name derives from the S-like shape of the curve (flatter at the beginning and end, steeper in the middle) produced on & project

that starts slowly, accelerates, and then tails off. Also a term for the cumulative likelihood distribution that is a result of a simulation, a tool of quantitative risk analysis.

- Statement of Work (SOW). A narrative description of products, services, or results to be supplied.
- SWOT Analysis (Strengths, Weaknesses, Opportunities, and Threats Analysis). This information gathering technique examines the project from the perspective of each project's strengths, weaknesses, opportunities, and threats to increase the breadth of the risks considered by risk management.
- Triple Constraint. A framework for evaluating competing demands. The triple constraint is often depicted as a triangle where one of the sides or one of the corners represent one of the parameters being managed by the project team.
- Value Engineering (VE). A creative approach used to optimize project life cycle costs, save time, increase profits, improve quality, expand market share, solve problems, and/or use resources more effectively.
- Work Breakdown Structure (WBS). A deliverable-oriented hierarchical decomposition of the work, to be executed by the project team to accomplish the project objectives and create the required deliverables. It organizes and defines the total scope of the project. Each descending level represents an increasingly detailed definition of the project work. The WBS is decomposed into work packages. The deliverable orientation of the hierarchy includes both internal and external deliverables. See also work package, control account, contract work, breakdown structure, and project summary work, breakdown structure.

Project Management Quotes

""A business that makes nothing but money is a poor business." – Henry Ford

"A plan that will not fit on one page cannot be understood." – Mark Ardis

"A good plan can help with risk analyses but it will never guarantee the smooth running of the project." – Bentley and Borman

"A plan is the map of the wise." – Adedeji B. Badiru

"A project is complete when it starts working for you, rather than you working for it." – Scott Allen

"A project without a critical path is like a ship without a rudder." – D. Meyer

"A task is not done until it is done." – Louis Frie

"A well-constructed project management
workshop should give people a solid foundation
to build on." – Bentley and Borman

"Add little to little and there will be a big pile" – Ovid

"All things are created twice; first mentally;
then physically. The key to creativity is to begin
with the end in mind, with a vision and a blue
print of the desired result." – Stephen Covey

"All things are created twice; first mentally;
then physically. The key to creativity is to begin
with the end in mind, with a vision and a blue
print of the desired result." – Stephen Covey

"An error does not become truth by reason of
multiplied propagation, nor does truth become error
because nobody sees it" – Mahatma Gandhi

"An intelligent person armed with a checklist is
no substitute for experience." – Joy Gumz

"An ounce of action is worth a ton of
theory." – Friedrich Engels

"Any Idiot can point out a problem …. A leader
is willing to do something about it! Leaders
solve problems!" – Tony Robbins

"Any fool can criticize, condemn, and complain, and
most fools do. But it takes character and self-control
to be understanding and forgiving." – Dale Carnegie

"As has been taught to teachers of the
Harvard Business School, the art of asking
good questions is often the most important
element of managerial tasks." – Parte Bose

"Assumption is the mother of all screw-ups." –
Wethern's Law of Suspended Judgement

"At times, project managers seem to forget that many
of the conventional forms, charts, and tables that
they must fill out are intended to serve as aids, not
punishments." – Mantel, Meredith, Shafer, and Sutton

"Before anything can be repeatable or reusable,
it must be usable." – Woody Williams

"Being a Project Manager is like being an artist,
you have the different colored process streams
combining into a work of art" – Greg Cimmarrusti

"Believe and act as if it were impossible to fail."

"Beware the time-driven project with an
artificial deadline." – M. Dobson

"Change is not made without inconvenience,
even from worse to better." – Samuel Johnson

"Communication is the root of everything
else." – Adedeji B. Badiru

"Data is like garbage. You'd better know what you are
going to do with it before you collect it." – Mark Twain

"Divide and conquer is the way to get
projects done." – Adedeji B. Badiru

"Do not repeat the tactics which have gained you
one victory, but let your methods be regulated by
the infinite variety of circumstances." – Sun Tzu

"Do not squander time, for that is the stuff
life is made of." – Benjamin Franklin

"Don't do anything you don't have to do." – Louis Fried

"Don't use a sledgehammer to crack a walnut, but equally don't agree important things informally where there is a chance of a disagreement later over what was agreed." – Colin Bentley

"Each completed task establishes certain parameters and imposes constraints on the next task." – Louis Fried

"Effective leaders help others to understand the necessity of change and to accept a common vision of the desired outcome." – John Kotter

"Ensure your documentation is short and sharp and make much more use of people-to-people communication." – Bentley and Borman

"Even if you are on the right track, you will get run over if you just sit there." – Will Rogers

"Event management is the same as for any project – the project plan needs to include an appropriate change control process." – Brenda Treasure

"Every moment is a golden one for him who has the vision to recognize it as such." – Henry Miller

"Every person takes the limits of their own field of vision for the limits of the world." – Arthur Schopenhauer

"External audits are routine in the financial area. I fail to understand why nonprofits don't use them more in the vital program area." – E. Stoesz

"First comes thought; then organization of that thought, into ideas and plans; then transformation of those plans into reality. The beginning, as you will observe, is in your imagination." – Napoleon Hill

"For a project plan to be effective it must equally address the parameters of 'activity time' and 'activity logic'. This logical relationship is required to model the effect schedule variance will have downstream in the project." – Rory Burke

"Get it done and put it behind you." – Adedeji B. Badiru

"Get the right people. Then no matter what all else you might do wrong after that, the people will save you. That's what management is all about." – Tom DeMarco

"Getting more things done requires focusing on fewer things to do." – Adedeji B. Badiru

"Give me six hours to chop down a tree and I will spend the first four sharpening the axe." – Abraham Lincoln

"Good business leaders create a vision, articulate the vision, passionately own the vision, and relentlessly drive it to completion." – Jack Welch

"Good judgment comes from experience, and experience comes from bad judgment." – Fred Brooks

"Good leaders do not take on all the work themselves; neither do they take all the credit." – Woody Williams

"Grass is always greener where you most need it to be dead." – Adedeji B. Badiru

"Great Works are performed not by Strength, but perseverance."

– Samuel Johnson (English author, 1709 - 1784)

"Haste makes waste just as rush makes
crash." – Adedeji B. Badiru

"He has half the deed done who has
made a beginning." – Horace

"He who has a 'why' to live for can bear with
almost any 'how'." – Friedrich Nietzsche

"I don't know the key to success, but the key to
failure is trying to please everyone" – Bill Cosby

"I have witnessed boards that continued to waste money
on doomed projects because no one was prepared to
admit they were failures, take the blame and switch
course. Smaller outfits are more willing to admit
mistakes and dump bad ideas." – Luke Johnson

"I hate housework! You do the dishes, and six months
later you have to start all over again." – Joan Rivers

"I like work. It fascinates me. I can sit and look
at it for hours." – Jerome Klapka Jerome

"I think there is something, more important
than believing. Action! The world is full of
dreamers, there aren't enough who will move
ahead and begin to take concrete steps to
actualize their vision." – W. Clement Stone

"I never dreamed about success. I
worked for it." – EsteeLauder

"If an IT project works the first time, it was a very
small and simple project." – Cornelius Fitchner

"If an IT project works the first time, it was
in your nightly dreams. Time to wake up
and get to work." – Cornelius Fitchner

"If everyone is thinking alike, someone isn't
thinking." – General George Patton Jr.

"If everything seems under control, you're not
going fast enough." – Mario Andretti

"If I have seen farther than others, it is because I was
standing on the shoulders of giants." – Isaac Newton

"If it is not documented, it doesn't exist. As
long information is retained in someone's head,
it is vulnerable to loss." – Louis Fried

"If money could just grow on trees, every miscreant
would have some." – Adedeji B. Badiru

"If you always blame others for your mistakes,
you will never improve." – Joy Gumz

"If you can't describe what you are doing
as a process, you don't know what you're
doing." – W. Edwards Deming

"If you don't start, it's certain you
won't arrive." – Zig Ziglar

"If you have never recommended canceling
a project, you haven't been an effective
project manager." – Woody Williams

"If you wait long enough, you won't have to
buy new technology." – Adedeji Badiru

"If, on your team, everyone's input is not
encouraged, valued, and welcome, why
call it a team?" – Woody Williams

"Imagination is more important than
knowledge." – Albert Einstein

"In NASA, we never punish error. We only
punish the concealment of error." – Al Siepert

"In poorly run projects, problems can go undetected
until the project fails. It's like the drip … drip … drip
of an leaky underground pipe. Money is being lost, but
you don't see it until there is an explosion." – Joy Gumz

"Innovative efforts should never report to line managers
charged with responsibility for ongoing operations. The
new project is an infant and will remain one for the
foreseeable future, and infants belong in the nursery.
The 'adults', that is, the executives in charge of existing
businesses or products will have neither the time nor
understanding for the infant." – Peter Drucker

"It doesn't take a lot of salt to add
the flavor" – Unknown

"It does not matter how slowly you go, so
long as you do not stop." – Confucius

"It is always easier to talk about change
than to make it." – Alvin Toffler

"It is better to know some of the questions
than all of the answers." – James Thurber

"It is not a question of how well each process works; the question is how well they all work together."
– Lloyd Dobyns and Clare Crawford-Mason

"It is useless to desire more time if you are already wasting what little you have." – James Allen

"It must be considered that there is nothing more difficult to carry out nor more doubtful of success nor more dangerous to handle than to initiate a new order of things." – Machiavelli

"It's easy to see, hard to foresee." – Benjamin Franklin

"It's not enough that we do our best; sometimes we have to do what's required." – Winston Churchill

"Keep your dreams alive. Understand to achieve anything requires faith and belief in yourself, vision, hard work, determination, and dedication. Remember all things are possible for those who believe." – Gail Devers

"Know when to cut your losses if necessary. Don't let your desire to succeed be the enemy of good judgment. If Napoleon had left Moscow immediately, he may have returned with a salvageable army." – Jerry Manas

"Lavish credit on anyone and everyone who helped you the least bit." – Tom Peters

"Let a plan be your project's guiding light." – Adedeji B. Badiru

"Life is like riding a bicycle. In order to keep your balance, you must keep moving." – Albert Einstein

"Like organic entities, projects have life cycles. From a slow beginning they progress to a buildup of size, then peak, begin a decline, and finally must be terminated. (Also, like other organic entities, they often resist termination.)" – Meredith and Mantel

"Make an extensive table of project 'deliverables'. Label one column 'as requested'. Create another column labeled 'could be'. Make each 'could be' wild and woolly!" – Tom Peters

"Management is doing things right; leadership is doing the right things." – Peter F. Drucker

"Momentum is a fragile force. Its worst enemy is procrastination. Its best friend is a deadline (think Election Day). Implication no. 1 (and there is no no. 2): Get to work! NOW!" – Tom Peters

"Most success depends on colleagues, on the team. People at the top have large egos, but you must never say 'I': it's always 'we'." – Frank Lampl

"My personal philosophy is not to undertake a project unless it is manifestly important and nearly impossible." – Edwin Land

"Never allow a person to tell you no who doesn't have the power to say yes." – Eleanor Roosevelt

"No major project is ever installed on time, within budget, with the same staff that started it." – Edwards, Butler, Hill and Russell

"No matter how good the team or how efficient the methodology, if we're not solving the right problem, the project fails." – Woody Williams

"No one can whistle a symphony. It takes
a whole orchestra." – H.E. Luccock

"Nobody knows how Honda is organized,
except that it uses lots of project teams and
is quite flexible." – Kenichi Ommae

"Of all the things I've done, the most vital is
coordinating the talents of those who work for us and
pointing them towards a certain goal." – Walt Disney

"Operations keeps the lights on, strategy provides
a light at the end of the tunnel, but project
management is the train engine that moves
the organization forward." – Joy Gumz

"Our focus on meaningful projects means
serving a useful social purpose while generating
high-quality profits." – Masimi Iijima

"People are more inclined to be drawn in if their
leader has a compelling vision. Great leaders help
people get in touch with their own aspirations
and then will help them forge those aspirations
into a personal vision." – John Kotter

"People buy into the leader before they buy
into the vision." – John C. Maxwell

"Pharmaceutical projects are like fresh fruit
– they depreciate if they are not tended to,
and they do poorly if sitting on the shelf with
long periods of inactivity." – R. Burns

"Planning without action is futile, action without
planning is fatal." – Cornelius Fitchner

"Plans are nothing; planning is everything."
– Dwight D. Eisenhower

"Plans are only good intentions unless they immediately degenerate into hard work." – Peter Drucker

"Plans are only good intentions unless they immediately degenerate into hard work." – Peter Drucker

"Plans are worthless, but planning is invaluable." – Peter Drucker

"PMs are the most creative pros in the world; we have to figure out everything that could go wrong, before it does." – Fredrik Haren

"Price is what you pay; value is what you get." – Warren Buffet

"Process for process sake is not good for goodness sake." – Lynn A. Edmark

"Project management can be defined as a way of developing structure in a complex project, where the independent variables of time, cost, resources and human behavior come together." – Rory Burke

"Project management is like juggling three balls – time, cost and quality. Program management is like a troupe of circus performers standing in a circle, each juggling-three balls and swapping balls from time to time." – G. Reiss

"Project management is the art of creating the illusion that any outcome is the result of a series of predetermined, deliberate acts when, in fact, it was dumb luck." – Harold Kerzner

"Project managers function as bandleaders who pull together their players each a specialist with individual score and internal rhythm. Under the leader's direction, they all respond to the same beat." – L.R. Sayles

"Project managers rarely lack organizational visibility, enjoy considerable variety in their day- to-day duties, and often have the prestige associated with work on the enterprise's high-priority objectives." – Meredith and Mantel

"Project proposals, business cases or cost benefit analyses are probably being massaged (either by underestimating costs or timeframes or by being very optimistic about the benefits) so projects will be approved." – Bentley and Borman

"Projects progress quickly until they become 90% complete; then remain at 90% complete forever." – Edwards, Butler, Hill and Russell

"Reconnaissance memoranda should always be written in the simplest style and be purely descriptive. They should never stray from their objective by introducing extraneous ideas." – Napoleon Bonaparte

"Resource is the engine of performance."
– Adedeji B. Badiru

"Rewards and motivation are an oil change for project engines. Do it regularly and often." – Woody Williams

"Running a project without a WBS is like going to a strange land without a roadmap." – J. Phillips

"Skills can be learned while experience must be earned." – Joy Gumz

"Some of the most flowery praise you hear on the subject of teams is only hypocrisy. Managers learn to talk a good game about teams even when they're secretly threatened by the whole concept." – Tom DeMarco

"Some things are better done than described." – Hunt and Thomas

"Teamwork works best." – Adedeji Badiru

"Tell me and I forget; Show me and I remember; Involve me and I understand." – Chinese Proverb

"Testing proves the presence of bugs but not their absence." – Woody Williams

"The conditions attached to a promise are forgotten and the promise is remembered." – Edwards, Butler, Hill and Russell

"The functional groups should not be allowed to stretch out the project for the sake of improvement, refinement, or the investigation of the most remote potential risk." – Meredith and Mantel

"The P in PM is as much about 'people management' as it is about 'project management'." – Cornelius Fichtner

"The project manager is expected to integrate all aspects of the project, ensure that the proper knowledge and resources are available when and where needed, and above all, ensure that the expected results are produced in a timely, cost-effective manner." – Meredith and Mantel

"The project manager must be able to develop a fully integrated information and control system to plan, instruct, monitor and control large amounts of data, quickly and accurately to facilitate the problem-solving and decision- making process." – Rory Burke

"The real problem is what to do with problem solvers after the problem is solved." – Gay Talese

"The reasonable man adapts himself to the world; the unreasonable one persists in trying to adapt the world to himself. Therefore, all progress depends on the unreasonable man." – George Bernard Shaw

"The testers won't break the system but the user who thinks the cd-rom drive as a drinks holder will." – Cornelius Fitchner

"The urgent problems are seldom the important ones." – Dwight D. Eisenhower

"There are two types of software : bad software and the next release." – Cornelius Fitchner

"There is nothing more perishable than an airline seat – unless it is time on a project." – Joy Gumz

"There is time for everything, and a season for each activity." – Ecclesiastes 3:1

"Things which matter most must never be at the mercy of things which matter least." – Goethe

"Think twice and act wise."

"This ad hoc approach to project management – coupled as it frequently is, with an on-the-job training philosophy – is pervasive. It is also pernicious." – Jack Meredith

"Time is like water in a sponge, the more you squeeze, the more you may get." – Chinese saying

"To get a project off the ground, tell a colleague it was their idea. They will put their heart and soul into making it successful." – T. Wouhra

"To get more done, try and do less." – Adedeji B. Badiru

"True motivation comes from achievement, personal development, job satisfaction, and recognition." – Frederick Herzberg

"Trying to manage a project without project management is like trying to play a football game without a game plan." – K. Tate

"Unengaged sponsor sinks the ship." – Angela Waner

"Unless commitment is made, there are only promises and hopes ... but no plans." –– Peter Drucker

"Vision is the art of seeing what is invisible to others." – Jonathan Swift

"Vision without action is a dream. Action without vision is simply passing the time. Action with Vision is making a positive difference." – Joel Barker

"We are what we repeatedly do. Excellence, therefore, is not an act but a habit." – Aristotle

"We cannot drive people; we must direct their development. Teach and lead." – Woody Williams

"We trained hard, but it seemed that every time we were beginning to form into teams we would be reorganized. I was to learn later in life that we tend to meet any new situation by reorganizing; and what a wonderful method it can be for creating the illusion of progress while producing confusion, inefficiency and demoralization." – Petronius Arbiter, 210 BC

"We will either find a way, or make one." –– Hannibal

"What is not on paper has not been said." – Anonymous

"What is truth today may be falsehood tomorrow. Never confuse your plan with truth." – Woody Williams

"What we are looking for is managers who are awake enough to alter the world as they find it, to make it harmonize with what they and their people are trying to accomplish." – Tom DeMarco

"What we learn from lessons learned is that we don?t learn from lessons learned." – T. Block

"Whatever we do must be in accord with human nature. We cannot drive people; we must direct their development. The general policy of the past has been to drive; but the era of force must give way to the era of knowledge, and the policy of the future will be to teach and lead, to the advantage of all concerned." – Henry L. Gantt

"When a risk occurs, with some ingenuity, this may open up an opportunity, and conversely when pursuing an opportunity there will be associated risks. Risks are generally deemed acceptable if the possible gains exceed the possible losses." – Rory Burke

"When debugging, novices insert corrective code; experts remove defective code." – Richard Pattis

"When end users get involved in the final stages of testing, light bulbs go on, and they often have an "aha" moment. Unfortunately, that is often too late." – Frank R. Parth

"When I dare to be powerful – to use my strength in the service of my vision, then it becomes less and less important whether I am afraid." – Audre Lorde

"When I dare to be powerful – to use my strength in the service of my vision, then it becomes less and less important whether I am afraid." – Audre Lorde

"When the territory and the map disagree, believe the territory." – Swiss Army Manual

"Whilst you can practice good project management without EVM, you cannot practice EVM effectively without good project management." – Steve Crowther

"Why do so many professionals say they are project managing, when what they are actually doing is fire fighting?" – Colin Bentley

"With vision there is no room to be frightened., No reason for intimidation. It's time to march forward! Let's be confident and positive!" – Charles R. Swindoll

"Working ten hour days allows you to fall behind twice as fast as you could working five hour days." – Issac Assimov

"You can only elevate individual performance by elevating that of the entire system." – W. Edwards Deming

"You can't keep it all in your head. Project control tools are an absolute necessity for the control of large projects." – Louis Fried

"You can't turn a herd of turtles into a twenty-mule work team." – L. Todryk

"You may con a person into committing to an unreasonable deadline, but you cannot bully them into meeting it." – Edwards, Butler, Hill, and Russell

"You must learn from the mistakes of others. You can't possibly live long enough to make them all yourself." – Sam Levenson

APPENDIX D

Project Management Proverbs and Phrases

Exercise Fairness
Exercise spirit of fairness at all times.

Use Concurrent Tasking
You may have to burn the candle at both ends to get more done.

Lighten Up
Lighten up and have fun while getting things done!

Exorcise Demons of Negativity
Overcome the insinuations of ANTS (Automatic Negative Thinkers). Negativity destroys hopes and aspirations.

Mind-Over-Matter Works
If you put your mind to it (positively), you can accomplish it.

Practice Healthy Lifestyle
Maintain a healthy lifestyle. Good health is essential for getting things done.

Embrace Life-long Learning
Learning new things creates new and exciting opportunities for getting things done effectively.

Do it the Right Way from the Start
There are both straight and narrow paths to getting things done. The shortest path may be the quickest way, but it may be paved with sticky tar of failure.

Stake a claim to success, by starting early
Get an early start and get ahead of the project game.

Delegate
Be courageous to delegate where it is appropriate and to the right people.

Perform some tasks with team approach
Teaming helps to share expertise, responsibilities, and resources to get things done.

Minimize multitasking
Although popular in theory, multitasking actually create more opportunities for errors and low quality of output.

Avoid procrastinating
Get on with what needs to be done; don't wait until the last minute. Making incremental gains on a task makes it easier to accomplish it without panic-button disruptions. Haste makes waste just as rush makes crash.

Prioritize
Prioritize and focus on the most important task at hand. Beware of time robbers.

Don't be a perfectionist
The pursuit of perfection is an impossible dream. Be realistic that there are limits to what can be accomplished.

Failure can be good
Don't be afraid to fail. Failure is often success turned inside out. Accept failure, if it comes, and learn from it.

Follow a plan, not a routine
Get out of a usual rote. Think and work outside the box to try new things.

Project Clichés

Declaration of a Project: Project management involves various interfaces within an organization. The exchange of information at each interface is crucial to the success of a project. The declaration below, the original source of which is unknown, takes a humorous look at the importance of information transfer and feedback in a project environment. The original composition has been modified here to fit the orientation of this book.

Declaration of Project Management (A Satire)

In the beginning there was the Project. With the Project, there was a Plan and a Specification. But the Plan was without form and the Specification was void. Thus, there was darkness upon the faces of the Engineers.

The Engineers, therefore, spoke unto their Project Leaders, "this is a crock of crap and we cannot abide the stink that abounds."

And the Project Leaders spoke unto their Unit Managers, "this is a crock of waste and we cannot abide the odor which abounds."

And the Unit Managers spoke unto their Sub-section Managers, "this is a vessel of waste and the odor is very offensive."

And the Sub-section Managers spoke unto their Section Managers, "this vessel is full of that which makes things grow and the characteristics thereof are exceedingly strong."

And the Section Managers spoke unto the General Manager, "the contents of this vessel are very powerful and will promote strong growth of the Company."

And the General Manager looked at the Project and saw that it was good. He, therefore, declared the Project fit for shareholders' consumption.

Project Management Proverbs

The stress of managing projects often calls for adages that aid project team members to see the lighter sides of their functions. The proverbs below represent a small sample of the various proverbs and sayings typically found in project management circles.

The same work under the same conditions will be estimated differently by ten different estimators or by one at ten different times.

You can bamboozle an engineer into committing to an unreasonable deadline, but you can't con him into meeting the deadline.

The more ridiculous the deadline, the more it costs to try to meet it.

A meeting is the confusion of one man multiplied by the number of people present.

The more desperate the situation, the more optimistic the project engineer.

Too few engineers on a project can't solve the problems; too many create more problems than they can solve.

You can freeze the users specifications, but you can't stop them from expecting.

The conditions of a promise are forgotten whenever the promise is remembered.

What you don't know is what really hurts you.

A user will tell you only what you ask about, and nothing more.

What is not on paper has not been said or heard.

No large project is ever installed on time, within budget, with the same staff that started it.

Projects progress quickly until they become 90 percent complete; then they remain at 90 percent complete forever.

A bad teacher lectures.

An average teacher teaches.

A good teacher demonstrates.

The best teacher inspires.

The rate of change of engineering projects often exceed the rate of progress.

Debugging engineering systems create new bugs that are unknown to engineers.

Progress reports are intended to show the lack of progress.

Murphy is alive and well in every project.

Peter's principle prevails in every organization.

Parkinson's law is every engineer's favorite.

Project Manager's Phrases

Project managers use insider phrases to convey ideas when dealing with project managers and clients. The phrases below offer hilarious interpretations of how project engineers communicate. A project manager must be able to read in between the lines to get an accurate picture of the status of a project. When a project is declared as being complete, it may mean that the implementation stage is about to begin.

Phrase 1: The concept was developed after years of intensive research.
Meaning: It was discovered by accident.

Phrase 2: The design will be finalized in the next reporting period.
Meaning: We haven't started this job yet, but we've got to keep the manager happy.

Phrase 3: A number of different approaches are being tried.
Meaning: We don't know where we're going yet, but we're moving.

Phrase 4: The project is slightly behind schedule due to unforeseen difficulties.
Meaning: We are working on something else.

Phrase 5: We have a close project coordination.
Meaning: Each project group does not know what the others are doing.

Phrase 6: Extensive report is being prepared on a fresh approach to the problem.
Meaning: We just hired three guys ... It will take them a while to figure out the problem.

Phrase 7: We've just had a major technological breakthrough.
Meaning: We are going back to the drawing board.

Phrase 8: Customer satisfaction is believed assured.
Meaning: We were so far behind schedule that the customer was happy to get anything at all from us.

Phrase 9: Preliminary operational tests were inconclusive.
Meaning: The poor thing blew up when we first tested it.

Phrase 10: Test results were extremely gratifying.
Meaning: It works; Boy, are we surprised.

Phrase 11: The entire concept will have to be abandoned.
Meaning: The only guy who understood the thing quit last week.

Phrase 12: We will get back to you soon.
Meaning: You will never hear from us again.

Phrase 13: Modifications are underway to correct certain minor difficulties.
Meaning: We threw the whole thing out and we are starting from scratch.

Phrase 14: We have completed an extensive review of your report.
Meaning: We have read the title page of your report.

Phrase 15: The drawings are in the mail.
Meaning: We are currently advertising to recruit someone to work on the designs.

Phrase 16: Your point of contact is currently on out-of-town assignment.
Meaning: The person you spoke with last week is no longer with the company.

Project Management Philosophies

1. Success, you will see it when you believe it . . . . . . "Everything is possible for him who believes." – Mark 9:23
2. You can get more done by doing less. If you tackle fewer things to do, you will get most of them done.
3. Just as prevention is better than cure, so is preemption better than correction. Anticipate and preempt sources of problems.
4. Know when to do what. Don't waste your daylight hours to do what you don't need daylight to do. On the other hand, "make hay while the sun shines."
5. What you can't do anything about, don't worry about. Worrying consumes time and keeps you from getting other things done.
6. Household junks accumulate to fill the available space. Strive to weed out unneeded junks in order to minimize non-value-adding junk-handling activities.
7. Plan, Execute, Learn, and Close projects.
8. Maintain a positive outlook. Things are never as bad as they seem. Even if they are bad, they could be worse.

9. Mind over matter works. If you put your mind to it, you can accomplish it.
10. Avoid ANTS (automatic negative thinkers) because they eat into your progress.
11. Accept and take risk. It is essential for accomplishing goals.
12. Recognize and ignore what you cannot change or accomplish. Focus on what you can change and do.
13. Never wait on work. Execute project schedule such that work waits on you.
14. Avoid "wait loss" by sequencing activities logically.
15. Embrace the concept of "everything in its place; a place for everything." It saves time when searching for tools.
16. Difficult times are the best times to embrace new challenges and learn new things.
17. Success is failure turned inside out. Learn and improve.
18. Keep things simple and focus on the fundamentals.
19. Measure and evaluate performance. It is the basis for continuous improvement.
20. Be proactive. Opportunity knocks, but it never enters on its own.
21. Create open communication channels and use them to achieve cooperation and task coordination.
22. It is crucial to use cooperative engagements in getting things done.
23. Take risk and go out on a limp sometimes. You cannot accumulate if you don't speculate.
24. Get all your facts before setting out to tackle unfamiliar tasks. Half of knowledge can be more harmful than no knowledge at all.
25. Be cheerful about your project. "A cheerful heart is good medicine." – Proverbs 17:22
26. Be positive and cheerful in all your undertakings. Each challenge is an opportunity to thrive.

Benefits of Project Challenges

Projects are built on challenges; and we should welcome them.
It is through challenges that we make mistakes.
It is through mistakes that we learn.

It is through learning that we improve.

It is through improvement that we achieve project success.

Tips for Personal Project Management

Managing a project is one thing, managing events that impede a project is another issue entirely. Little things that we fail to manage at home or at work can significantly impact project success. A good example is household tips. Proactive routine maintenance of household assets can preempt time-consuming worries and repairs later on. The time, thus saved, can then be used for more productive project activities be it at home or at work. Self-help guides are replete with tips on household management and home improvement. But such tips often focus only on the cost saving aspects as well as convenience of the home owner. In this book we extend those familiar reasons to include benefits of better project management within or outside the home. Time saved at home will be time available for accomplishments at work. Common examples of household tasks, whether you Do-It-Yourself (DIY) or not, include the following:

1. Change furnace and air-conditioning filters as recommended by the manufacturer. This preempts breakdowns that may cause worry time, repair cost, repair time, and diversion of efforts from productive activities.
2. Replace door locks when you move into a new house, especially previously owned homes. This preempts security issues that may impede productive engagements later on.
3. Learn location of main water cut-off. In case of water accident, prior knowledge of the location will save time and preempts the need to run around helter-skelter trying to solve the problem. This facilitates effectiveness and efficiency in responding to home emergencies.
4. Proactively maintain the family vehicle. Doing the manufacturer-recommended maintenance proactively means that you do it at your own convenience sans pressure. This preempts having to deal with emergency breakdowns which may occur at the most

inconvenient times. Time, thus saved, can be diverted to more productive project engagements. The idea of "if it ain't broke, don't fix it" does not help effective project management because when it finally "breaks," all hell may break loose.

Project Management for Kids

It is never too early to get kids to start appreciating the power of project management. Kids can learn to apply the basic tools and techniques of project management when helping with domestic chores are home, class projects at school, or group projects around the community. Kids can learn age-appropriate principles of project management through formal programs and play-oriented fairs. A good example is a project execution show organized by Home Depot at a downtown fair in Dayton, Ohio in the Summer of 2013. I had the pleasure of taking a nine-year-old grand niece, Miss Bisi Omosanya, to the show, where she, with the help of the booth attendants, built a Valentine Holder. She was so proud of herself that she subsequently asked questions about how, why, when, and who of executing small projects. Her proud moment is depicted in the photo collage below.

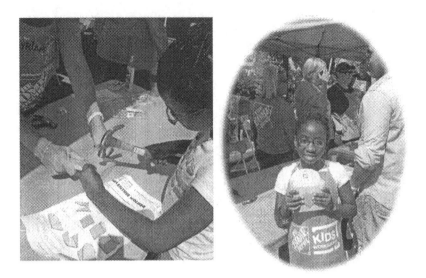

Having been exposed to the principles, Bisi constantly asked me for little projects we could do together around the house, the garage, and the basement. She so completely embraced the concept of family project management that she earned the special poem that I wrote for her below.

Bisi Like Busy

Bisi like busy is Bisi the busy.
Bisi likes being busy; and
She is always busy.
Bisi wakes up early just to be busy;
Bisi wakes up before Grandpa to help him with his busy day;
Bisi likes going to school, where she can be her Bisi self; always busy.
Bisi loves going to festivals, where she likes rides, just to be busy.
Up and down Bisi goes on a ride, being busy again.
Bisi the busy; she is always busy.
Little busy is a Big competitor for Grandpa's busy ways.
Bisi must be a busy bee with her project management.

50 Ways to Improve Your Project

1. Abide by rules of the project.
2. Align corporate projects with organizational needs.
3. Align home projects with family needs.
4. Allocate sufficient resources to meet project objectives.
5. Be good, so that you can receive goodness from others.
6. Be specific with requirements.
7. Check on project milestones.
8. Commit to whatever you are doing.
9. Communicate to solicit cooperation.
10. Cooperate so that you may receive cooperation in return.
11. Coordinate with others so that the load can be shared.
12. Define goals clearly upfront.
13. Delegate so that other may learn the path to success.
14. Do not cut corners; corners can come back around.
15. Document the project for future reference.
16. Don't despair; there is success at the end of the project tunnel.
17. Embrace ethics as a platform for project success.
18. Embrace new ideas.
19. Enjoy leisure as a break from project monotony.
20. Evaluate consequences of project actions.
21. Focus on the end goal.

22. Get organized.
23. Homestead for personal projects.
24. Integrate project outcomes with the operating environment.
25. Justify each time or resource expenditure on the project.
26. Keep project scope within reason.
27. Know that time is everything; once lost, it cannot be recovered.
28. Make accountability a requirement for project execution.
29. Manage yourself as a critical resource for your project.
30. Measure everything to provide a metric of assessment.
31. Network with potential project allies.
32. Operate lean and cut out fluff.
33. Place tools where they belong.
34. Plan and plan again.
35. Practice continuous improvement.
36. Preempt project problems by asking "what-if" questions.
37. Promise only what you can deliver.
38. Question everything with a constructive open mind.
39. Recognize that there is always room for improvement.
40. Re-plan when plan is not going well.
41. Schedule each activity so that it can get done.
42. Set standards so that your project will have a target.
43. Sleep enough so that you can be rejuvenated for your project.
44. Take care of your health as a project asset; no health no success.
45. Take corrective actions at the earliest opportunity.
46. Take responsibility for what you are responsible for.
47. Treat your people well; they are your most enduring project resource.
48. View everything as a project.
49. Observe safety requirements; accidents divert attention.
50. Simplify your process.

Deji Badiru is a professor of Systems Engineering at the Air Force Institute of Technology (AFIT). He was previously head of Industrial & Information Engineering at the University of Tennessee in Knoxville, and former professor of industrial engineering and Dean of University College at the University of Oklahoma. He is a registered professional engineer. He is a fellow of the Institute of Industrial Engineers and a Fellow of the Nigerian Academy of Engineering. He holds BS in Industrial Engineering, MS in Mathematics, and MS in Industrial Engineering from Tennessee Technological University, and Ph.D. in Industrial Engineering from the University of Central Florida. His areas of expertise include mathematical systems modeling, project modeling, analysis, management and control, economic analysis, productivity analysis and improvement. He is the author of several books and technical journal articles. He is a member of several professional societies and honor associations. He has won awards for his teaching, research, and managerial accomplishments.

INDEX